Cambridge Elements

Elements in Data Rights and Wrongs
edited by
Megan Richardson
University of Melbourne
Rachelle Bosua
Deakin University
Damian Clifford
Australian National University
Jake Goldenfein
University of Melbourne
Jeannie Marie Paterson
University of Melbourne
Julian Thomas
RMIT University

DATA ACCESS AND AI EXPLAINABILITY

Frank Pasquale
Cornell Tech and Cornell Law School

Shaftesbury Road, Cambridge CB2 8EA, United Kingdom

One Liberty Plaza, 20th Floor, New York, NY 10006, USA

477 Williamstown Road, Port Melbourne, VIC 3207, Australia

314–321, 3rd Floor, Plot 3, Splendor Forum, Jasola District Centre, New Delhi – 110025, India

103 Penang Road, #05–06/07, Visioncrest Commercial, Singapore 238467

Cambridge University Press is part of Cambridge University Press & Assessment, a department of the University of Cambridge.

We share the University's mission to contribute to society through the pursuit of education, learning and research at the highest international levels of excellence.

www.cambridge.org
Information on this title: www.cambridge.org/9781009627368

DOI: 10.1017/9781009627351

© Frank Pasquale 2025

This publication is in copyright. Subject to statutory exception and to the provisions of relevant collective licensing agreements, with the exception of the Creative Commons version the link for which is provided below, no reproduction of any part may take place without the written permission of Cambridge University Press & Assessment.

An online version of this work is published at doi.org/10.1017/9781009627351 under a Creative Commons Open Access license CC-BY-NC 4.0 which permits re-use, distribution and reproduction in any medium for non-commercial purposes providing appropriate credit to the original work is given and any changes made are indicated. To view a copy of this license visit https://creativecommons.org/licenses/by-nc/4.0

When citing this work, please include a reference to the DOI 10.1017/9781009627351

First published 2025

A catalogue record for this publication is available from the British Library

ISBN 978-1-009-62736-8 Hardback
ISBN 978-1-009-62737-5 Paperback
ISSN 2976-7520 (online)
ISSN 2976-7512 (print)

Cambridge University Press & Assessment has no responsibility for the persistence or accuracy of URLs for external or third-party internet websites referred to in this publication and does not guarantee that any content on such websites is, or will remain, accurate or appropriate.

For EU product safety concerns, contact us at Calle de José Abascal, 56, 1°, 28003 Madrid, Spain, or email eugpsr@cambridge.org

Data Access and AI Explainability

Elements in Data Rights and Wrongs

DOI: 10.1017/9781009627351
First published online: August 2025

Frank Pasquale
Cornell Tech and Cornell Law School
Author for correspondence: Frank Pasquale, fp269@cornell.edu

Abstract: As managers digitize judgment using AI, their evaluations of persons risk imposing benefits and burdens in opaque and unaccountable ways. A wide range of harms may occur when access to one's personal data (and meaningful information about its use) is denied. Key data access rights and AI explainability guarantees in US and EU law are designed to ameliorate the harms caused by irresponsible digitization, but their definition and range of application is contested. A robust policy evaluation framework will be needed to inform the proper level and scope of information access, as regulators clarify the contours of such rights and guarantees. By revealing the stakes of data access, this Element offers a useful evaluative framework for those interpreting and applying laws of data protection and AI explainability. This title is also available as Open Access on Cambridge Core.

Keywords: data protection, data access, AI explainability, policy evaluation, reputation

© Frank Pasquale 2025

ISBNs: 9781009627368 (HB), 9781009627375 (PB), 9781009627351 (OC)
ISSNs: 2976-7520 (online), 2976-7512 (print)

Contents

1 Introduction   1

2 Uses and Misuses of Data   4

3 The Growth and Contested Scope of Access Rights Initiatives   17

4 The Future of Information Access Rights: Empowering Civil Society and Social Reform   47

5 Conclusion: Increasing the Dimensionality of Policy Evaluation with Respect to Data Protection   57

References   59

1 Introduction

> [I]t is becoming much easier for recordkeeping systems to affect people than for people to affect record-keeping systems. ... Although there is nothing inherently unfair in trading some measure of privacy for a benefit, both parties to the exchange should participate in setting the terms
>
> (U.S. Department of Health, Education & Welfare, 1973)

If a self-checkout machine at a store categorizes you as a "potential threat," and calls the police, should you be able to learn why you were classified in this way – or at least what data was used to make the determination? If an algorithmic lender decides to raise your credit card interest rate based on your cell phone usage patterns, should you be able to inspect the data, and demand some accounting for why you need to pay more? In the most general terms: if a company gathers data about you and makes a decision about you, should you be entitled to access the data and learn how the decision was made?

Answers to questions like these will help determine the fairness and intelligibility of commercial life in years to come. Expansive deployments of predictive analytics, artificial intelligence (AI), and "big data" to judge consumers and workers have highlighted new uses of a venerable aspect of fair information practices: data subjects' right to access information collected about them, including how the data was used to judge them.

These rights have global relevance. They have long been part of sectoral United States (US) and general European Union (EU) data protection regimes governing private sector data collection. Indeed, the Organization for Economic Cooperation and Development (OECD) included "information participation" as one of its original eight Fair Information Practice Principles (FIPPs) in its Guidelines on the Protection of Privacy and Transborder Flows of Personal Data (OECD, 1980). Australia has long offered such protections in financial contexts, and its 2023 Privacy Act Review has proposed a "right for individuals to request meaningful information about how substantially automated decisions with legal or similarly significant effect are made" (Attorney-General's Department, 2023). Similarly, Japan's Act on the Protection of Personal Information grants citizens the right to review data held about them by businesses.

There is a vast secondary literature on the US and EU legal regimes of data access, and they will be the focus of the third section of this Element. However, Sections 2 and 4 aim for a wider relevance, as they draw from case studies and policy arguments that present live issues globally. All sections develop the importance of two intertwined, but distinct clusters of rights in commercial contexts. The first is data access: the ability to inspect and copy for one's own purposes, the data held about oneself by an entity. The second is explainability: the ability to demand some meaningful information from an entity about how it used the data it held to profile or make a decision about oneself. While such decisions have been automated in many contexts for decades, this Element addresses AI explainability because both predictive and generative AI are likely to play increasingly important roles in ranking, rating, and categorizing persons.

Persons may exercise data access rights when they review a credit report for errors, for example, or request their medical records. The right to an explanation may be valuable in many contexts, ranging from banking to hiring to house-letting – wherever an algorithmic characterization of a person's reliability or qualifications results in (or informs) a consequential decision about them. Through the rest of the 2020s and beyond, both regulators and courts around the world will be interpreting the scope of existing law on access rights. Jurisdictions internationally will weigh the advantages and disadvantages of tighter and looser requirements for data access and AI explainability.

All this legal activity has both spurred – and has been spurred by – activism. Workers have rallied around data access rights to help level the gig economy playing field. Consumers have used their data to launch legal challenges against allegedly fraudulent securities sales. Data access has been of great use to many. Meanwhile, the businesses that are the target of data access and explainability laws are fiercely lobbying to limit their scope. They worry about being saddled with extensive (and expensive) obligations to document and explain their decisions. Some experts even assert that, as computational methods become more complex, it is impossible to keep track of all the data used to generate AI outputs, let alone explaining the results of the systems they deploy.

To help the reader better understand these and other debates in the data protection field, this Element will explore the virtues and limits of data access and explainability. Section 2 sets the stage for the discussion by establishing the empirical and normative foundations for renewed attention to information access rights (IARs) – a blanket term covering both data access and explainability. Advanced forms of computing are increasingly digitizing personal evaluations in ways that are difficult to understand. These advances raise at least two sets of normative concerns. First, algorithmic judgments may be premised on inaccurate or inappropriate digitized records. Second, even if all the data processed is accurate and relevant to the decision at hand, the AI may be discriminatory against certain groups. Access rights respond to these concerns by giving those suspicious of automated decision-making systems access to the data, and some aspects of the algorithms, being used to judge them, so they can check for inaccurate, illegal, or discriminatory data uses.

Despite the need for IARs to expose inaccuracy and discrimination, their scope is surprisingly limited in some contexts, and uncertain in others, as Section 3 demonstrates, using case studies from the US and EU. For instance, the U.S. Fair Credit Reporting Act fails to require disclosure of data used in many types of algorithmic lending. Guidance on the U.S. Equal Credit Opportunity Act's requirements for proper "adverse impact" notices remains underdeveloped. The field is even more wide open in California, where a relatively new government agency (the California Consumer Protection Agency (CPPA)) will be interpreting some critically important, but vague, statutory terms as it establishes the scope of access rights. In Europe, at least one credit bureau has asserted its trade secrecy rights to blunt the impact of General Data Protection Regulation (GDPR) requirements for transparency. The E.U. AI Act has declared credit scoring to be a "high-risk" form of AI, so it should impose additional requirements. But it remains to be seen whether these will also be defused by assertions of trade secrecy or other defenses.

As these regulatory processes continue, many data-intensive business enterprises have advanced narrow interpretations of IARs by highlighting the costs of data protection rules in general, and IARs in particular. Economically focused policy evaluations have tended to emphasize and quantify the cost of data protection regulations, while only episodically discussing their benefits. Section 4 aims to help right this balance, by developing a fuller accounting of the benefits of access rights, premised on more capacious methods of policy evaluation. Information access rights help alleviate the risk and anxiety attendant on many forms of opaque and unaccountable automated decision-making. Data access and explainability spark forms of public knowledge and inquiry that are vital to competitive markets and democratic societies. Unions, journalists, and civil society organizations are capitalizing on access requests to expose troubling practices. The net effect is to build a new form of intellectual infrastructure for numerous efforts to address unfair power differentials in the data economy. The long-term hope is that data access will empower groups to identify and redress data-driven harms.

Before diving in to the substance, I should note several limits to the present inquiry. First, although state accumulation of data is a critical issue I have addressed in prior work like *The Black Box Society*, I do not do so here. The bodies of law that have developed around state accountability for data and AI decision-making are in many ways distinct from those surrounding the private sector activities which are the focus of this Element. Second, this work is focused on the interaction between data subjects and data controllers and processors, rather than state-required disclosures from the latter. While general disclosure requirements pursuant to laws like the Digital Services Act have greatly assisted public understanding of online life, they are better understood as corporate obligations, rather than the type of individualized rights focused on here. Third, while addressing the data policy (and policy evaluation) concerns that are near-universal, this Element focuses its legal analysis on specific provisions of US and EU IARs. This is because the legal analysis of Section 3 is not meant to provide a universal template of interpretation, but rather, is intended as a way of documenting (a) how laws address the problems identified in Section 2, and (b) how their interpretation or revision raises the types of policy evaluation controversies addressed in Section 4.

Having set forth these provisos, we are now in a good position to explore the harms an unregulated data market can pose, and how legislators and regulators might address them in an informed manner. A richer policy evaluation framework for the law of data access and explainability must be rooted in the full range of concerns that have led to governmental regulation of corporations' evaluations of persons. These concerns are the focus of Section 2.

2 Uses and Misuses of Data

Access rights are gaining increasing attention and support at an important inflection point in the digital economy. An increasing variety, volume, and velocity of data are influencing evaluations of persons in many sectors (Pasquale, 2020: 119–123). For example, life insurers may use unusual and unexpected data sources in order to make underwriting decisions about whom to cover, and for how much (Regalbuto, 2019).[1] Information like tone of voice, or cell phone use patterns, may be used to characterize a person as being more likely than others to suffer from mental health issues (Marks, 2021). As intermediaries like YouTube, Facebook, and Instagram structure their users' time online, they are making personalized judgments about what to show and what to hide based on myriad sources of data.

Many persons and advocacy groups want access to the data being used to judge them. Persons fear being misjudged on the basis of inaccurate or inappropriate data. Kafkaesque stories of inaccurate data-dogging persons have raised public awareness. The quotidian inconvenience of (and sometimes extreme frustration at) disputing an invalid medical debt, or struggling to correct a credit report, has

---

[1] The New York Department of Financial Services documented "the emergence of unconventional sources or types of external data available to insurers, including within algorithms and predictive models" (Regalbuto, 2019). For imaginative narrative extrapolations of how such trends may continue, see Kai-Fu Lee and Chen Qiufan's *AI 2041* (Lee & Chen, 2021). I have promoted the value of considering such narratives in policy contexts (Pasquale, 2023), particularly as they help regulators anticipate and discourage troubling uses of technology, and promulgate rules to stop them, rather than merely punishing wrongdoers ex post after damage has been done.

motivated wide interest in increasing algorithmic accountability – including revealing the data fed into digitized evaluations of persons, and meaningful information about what data mattered most to the evaluation.

This section begins by describing pattern-matching characteristics of machine learning (ML) systems (Section 2.1). To suggest the wide array of data sources available, and the discretion enjoyed by programmers, Section 2.2 describes in detail the steps a firm might take in order to automate credit determinations. The rest of Section 2 details key normative challenges posed by this digital transition (2.3). Major concerns include the use of inaccurate and inappropriate data, and discrimination against marginalized groups.

2.1 How Models, Algorithms, and AI Digitize Judgment

From the computational perspective of predictive AI, the task of ranking and rating applicants for loans, jobs, college admissions, and other opportunities, is a problem of statistical pattern recognition. While each of these spheres of judgment relies on distinct forms of data and prediction, financial scoring and prediction has been of particularly long-standing, and is accordingly well-studied. This section treats such financial scoring as a case study to introduce important dilemmas and policy concerns that are generally prevalent in digitized judgment.

Early forms of credit evaluation focused on narrative accounts of creditworthiness, and such narratives are still decisive in limited contexts (Pasquale & Kiriakos, 2025). However, scoring recorded behavior allowed faster evaluation at scale, and largely displaced narrative modes. For example, in a very simple scoring model, an applicant might start with a base score of 800 points, and then lose 25 points for each late payment or "credit inquiry" reported to a credit bureau (Siddiqi, 2006; Bolder, 2018). The resulting number of points was much easier to apprehend and compare than a story of why the late payments occurred. By the mid twentieth century, credit bureaus had gathered records of persons' repayment histories from various sources (Siddiqi, 2006). They then sold access to these credit histories to lenders (Dixon & Gellman, 2014: 81). By the 1960s, a firm called "Fair Isaac" had begun to assign point values to different aspects of persons' credit histories (Gunter, 2000).

A credit scoring system based on past repayment history and a few other simple variables (like the percentage of applicant's extant credit used at the time of application for new credit) was seen by many as a major advance over past, more qualitative judgments. Advocates for scoring touted machines' cool objectivity. A series of works has characterized ML generally as unburdened by the emotions, bias, and "noise" afflicting unaided human cognition (Wu &

Zhang, 2016; Kahneman et al., 2021; Sunstein, 2022; but see Pasquale, 2018, responding to Wu & Zhang and similar work). Nevertheless, the relatively transparent scoring system failed to qualify tens of millions of persons for credit, many of whom could have easily paid back the loans. Some did not have a long enough repayment history, facing a familiar chicken-and-egg problem: They could not reliably repay a loan, without first getting a loan, which depended on a credit history, which in turn depended on a repayment history.[2] Other "thin file" borrowers found similar problems in their efforts to access credit.

The answer, for advocates of ML, was to search for patterns of common characteristics among (1) those presently rejected and (2) reliable or profitable applicants generally. These can be very different forms of optimization. For example, a borrower who takes out a very small loan, but who pays a great deal of interest and late fees, may be more profitable than most other applicants, even if the borrower ultimately defaults. This question of multiple optimization strategies highlights the questions of values that are often elided in the business literature on AI deployment.

Persons who repay their debts on time may be more likely to drive within 10 miles of the speed limit, buy detergent in bulk, or limit their time on social media – all factors which were not reflected in older credit reports. A recognition system capable of identifying a critical mass of such similarities among "digital doubles" stands a strong chance of predicting credit risk well, without the traditional data necessary for older scoring systems. As one former Google executive (and later CEO of ZestFinance) put it, "all data is credit data" (Zax, 2012). There may be signs and signals of creditworthiness far afield from traditional credit reporting data, presenting new "matches" of applicants with preferred and suspect patterns of behavior.

The precise mechanism for this matching can vary. Different types of ML may be deployed, granting considerable discretion to analysts. For example, supervised learning involves "learning from a training set of labeled examples provided by a knowledgeable external supervisor" (Sutton & Barto, 2019). There are many databases of credit experience available, with characteristics recorded about each borrower. When simple binaries are applied to each file (defaulter/non-defaulter, or profitable/unprofitable), an algorithm may "learn" the characteristics of desirable borrowers – or at least what data correlates with

---

[2] Note that public student loans in the US help solve this problem for many because they are guaranteed issue, with very little exclusionary underwriting. Co-signers can also help overcome this hurdle. Thus credit access is not merely a problem of accurately predicting repayment, but also of institutional design to make repayment more likely, including via provision of loan forgiveness terms – a feature of many student lending systems.

desirability. By contrast, "unsupervised learning" is "typically about finding structure hidden in collections of unlabeled data" (Sutton & Barto, 2019: 12). In the credit case, this may involve separating files into various binaries, and later review may reveal a "default/non-default" binary even if only a fraction of files have actually been labeled by default status. A third type of ML, reinforcement learning, involves "trying to maximize a reward signal instead of trying to find hidden structure" (Sutton & Barto, 2019: 12).[3] As Thomas Gilbert and co-authors explain,

> The goal of reinforcement learning [RL] is to design a rule for choosing actions based on observations about the system. This rule is called a behavioral policy, and it is designed (or learned) by using data toward the goal of optimizing a cumulative reward. For example, by probing the characteristics and viewing history of users, an RL agent could learn what videos to recommend to particular people to maximize their time on a given website or application. (Gilbert et al., 2022: 6)

Note that, as researchers move from the natural to the social world, the normative valence of "success" in such operations changes. A reinforcement learning algorithm situated in a learning health care system that improves in its ability to identify dangerous cancers is an unqualified good. When similar technology lures (or even addicts) YouTube viewers with a steady diet of sensationalism and extremism, or finds the optimal variable reward mechanism to promote gambling, its social effects are suspect (Schüll, 2012; Gilbert et al., 2022: 19).[4] Nor is an algorithm for financial inclusion likely to be societally optimal if it targets potential customers who will profit a bank by constantly paying late fees, or covering loan payments with more loans from other sources.

Machine learning has achieved some extraordinary breakthroughs to promote human well-being, particularly in the medical field (Topol, 2019). But given its dependence on necessarily partial and time-bound data sets, ML can exhibit surprising fragility, particularly in the social (as opposed to natural) world (Eykholt et al., 2018; Bender et al., 2021).[5] Thus, we should carefully consider the potential slippages between natural science models of ML and the

---

[3] As these authors put it: "To obtain a lot of reward, a reinforcement learning agent must prefer actions that it has tried in the past and found to be effective in producing reward ... But to discover such actions, it has to try actions that it has not selected before. The agent has to exploit what it has already experienced in order to obtain reward, but it also has to explore in order to make better action selections in the future."

[4] Natasha Dow Schüll (Schüll, 2012) also describes how methods of maximizing "time on machine" for gamblers have been explored by technologists in other fields.

[5] For example, a self-driving car's "vision" system may interpret a stop sign as a "45 miles per hour" sign if some pieces of tape are placed on the sign (Bender et al., 2021), illustrating the dangers of such infirmities in LLMs.

new human science of ML-driven evaluation. There are clear binaries between, say, normal and abnormal tissue. When it comes to persons, ambiguities abound. Is the optimal bank client one who always pays on time, for example, or one who is constantly paying late fees? Regulations meant to guarantee sustainable debt loads are a belated effort to restrain the latter, fee-driven business strategy.

Similar issues arise in hiring and employment. Unions and management have clashed over what are fair, reasonable, and accurate ways of evaluating job performance (O'Neil, 2016).[6] There have been many calls for more worker and union participation (Mandinaud & Ponce del Castillo, 2024). Optimal qualifications for a successful applicant are also highly contestable. Even more troublingly, AI can reinforce old forms of bias unintentionally. If a firm's leadership is largely male, for example, markers of maleness may be taken as markers of success by its algorithms (Dastin, 2018). But before addressing such normative issues systematically in Section 2.3, it is helpful to give more detail about how a particular firm might use ML systems to come to a decision about an applicant.

2.2 A Consumer Scoring Case Study

Discussions of access rights to data can become very abstract, very quickly. To assist in grounding the normative and legal analysis that follows, a heuristic hypothetical evaluation system should prove helpful. Consider, for instance, an algorithmic lender which took the following actions to develop its ML model, and its decision about a particular borrower, referred to here for the sake of convenience as Alice:

(1) The firm compiled a training data set comprised of 500 data points about 100,000 persons:

  a. 80,000 of whom fully paid off their loans without late payments or defaults,
  b. 10,000 of whom had late payments, and
  c. 10,000 of whom defaulted.

(2) These 500 data points included:

  a. Websites visited, based on IP address,
  b. Food purchased at any of ten grocery store chains,

---

[6] Cathy O'Neill in *Weapons of Mass Destruction* (O'Neil, 2016), for instance, describes a faulty Value Added Model used to evaluate teachers' performance in Houston that led to some unfair firings.

c. Music playlists on a music streaming service, and
   d. The following public records scraped by the lender:
      i. Voting
      ii. Arrests
(3) The firm tried to accumulate the same data points from all applicants.
(4) When applicants' data was gathered, it was subsequently "cleaned," in order to eliminate implausible results. In Alice's case, a data point indicating fifty visits to the *New York Times* website (nytimes.com) in one day was eliminated as an "outlier," on the assumption that the site automatically reloaded many times due to a browser glitch. No person in the training data set had visited it more than twenty times in one day, so a data scientist programmed the algorithm to eliminate any site-visit metric above forty as a likely page refreshing error.
(5) When Alice applied, the firm was able to collect 450 of the 500 desired data points for her application.
(6) The firm attributed the other 50 data points to Alice based on characteristics of persons in its training data set who lived within 10 miles of her.
(7) The firm ran two supervised learning, two reinforcement learning, and one unsupervised ML models to determine whether Alice's profile was most similar to the profile of persons within groups 1a, 1b, or 1c above.
(8) Four of the models placed Alice in group 1a, predicting she would not default or have any late payments.[7] The unsupervised model placed Alice in group 1c, predicting default.
(9) Out of an abundance of caution, the firm denied Alice's application, based on internal guidance documents that restricted grants of credit to persons classified as 1c by any of the firm's models.[8]

Assume, for now, that Alice received no information about the grounds for the decision. The example reveals several junctures at which even highly professionalized and technically competent forms of ML, may lead to troubling

---

[7] For the range of types of models that could be used in this scenario, see Maisa Cardoso Aniceto (Aniceto et al., 2020) describing Support Vector Machine, Decision Trees, Bagging, AdaBoost, and Random Forest models.

[8] Compare James Grimmelmann & Daniel Westreich (Grimmelmann & Westreich, 2017) (including a nuanced hiring hypothetical where an algorithm identifies certain characteristics correlated with higher job performance). See Sandra Wachter (Wachter, 2022) for a thoughtful reform proposal aimed at curbing discrimination against "algorithmic groups." For simplicity's sake, discussions of this hypothetical will assume the lender is simply trying to avoid late payments and defaults, rather than (for example) maximizing overall revenues by luring some borrowers to pay massive interest payments and late fees. This simplification, while risking a presentation of the financial industry in a more benign light than it may deserve, dramatizes the bluntness of many optimization metrics.

practices (Lehr & Ohm, 2017).[9] For example, the practice of data cleaning (to remove outliers) may be standard and generally effective, but in this case, it did misrepresent Alice's online life to the relevant algorithms. Arrest records may seem like just another data point to an analyst in search of more correlations, but they are highly questionable sources of data for credit determinations, given a long history of discriminatory policing practices (concentrating surveillance and enforcement in minority neighborhoods) (Richardson et al., 2019). In other words: data sets that may seem highly probative and informative to a data scientist trying to predict future behavior, may be riddled with bias, inaccuracies, or other problems. As Section 2.3 shows, these concerns are generalizable to other digitized judgments.

2.3 Perils of the Digitization of Judgment

Algorithmic and quantitative methods have an uneasy place in evaluative judgments. They promise to bring rigor and objectivity to opportunities too often afflicted by subjective caprice. However, they have also accelerated predictable injustices. As Fourcade & Healy have eloquently argued in their *The Ordinal Society*, the ranking, rating, and classification of people, institutions, and cultural production makes contemporary life more convenient and competitive, opaque and open, rigorous and random (Fourcade & Healy, 2024). Their account unravels key paradoxes of digitality, particularly computation's role in simultaneously promoting democratization and hierarchy.

Law and policy can reduce the negative effects of the digitization of judgment without undermining its most positive effects. The creators and users of algorithms promote rigor in the administration of evaluative processes, but must themselves be held accountable for quantitative methods' failures and biases (Nissenbaum, 1996). Researchers have exposed firms showing women ads for lower-paying jobs, discriminating against the aged, and deploying deceptive "dark patterns" to trick consumers into online subscriptions (Gibbs, 2015; Angwin et al., 2017; Warner, 2019).

Sections 2.3.1–2.3.3 categorize these and similar problems. They do not exhaust normative critiques of opaque data collection and usage. A more complete account would likely explore the undermining of collective action that results from opaque data systems, and the distrust in institutions such systems provoke. Opaque data systems also threaten democracy. Nevertheless, the typology of inaccurate, inappropriate, and discriminatory data provides ample normative foundations for the law and policy to be explored in Section 3.

---

[9] Drilling down to discuss the nuts and bolts of data gathering and analysis is an important step toward more sophisticated legal treatments of machine learning regulation.

2.3.1 Inaccurate Data

There are numerous legitimate and fair sources and uses of data for profiling purposes. However, businesses will be tempted to use data whose provenance they cannot be certain about. Information freely scraped from the public internet, for example, is both exceedingly cheap and frequently dubious (Birhane et al., 2021). Inaccurate data is surprisingly common (Federal Trade Commission, 2013).[10] When firms compile inaccurate data about individuals, the errors have reverberating effects, since one inaccurate data point may proliferate through hundreds of databases given the ease of digital transfers of data (Citron, 2010).[11]

Given the secrecy shrouding most corporate data troves from public scrutiny, it is impossible to accurately estimate the prevalence of inaccurate commercial data generally. However, case studies by determined researchers have illuminated some corners of these largely opaque business practices. Sociologist Mary Ebeling has offered a particularly thoughtful perspective on the dilemmas caused by poorly regulated data exchange (Ebeling, 2016). Ebeling visited her doctor several times before suffering a miscarriage. When companies marketed baby products to her for years after the miscarriage, she began to call all the marketing agencies that had reached out to her. Compiling clueless or obfuscatory responses, she exposed the so-called wizardry of big data marketing as a baffling amalgam of unreliable inferences and impenetrable bureaucracies:

> Over the months and years since I lost my baby in March 2011, I have received more than eighty separate email solicitations, social media advertisements, phone calls, mailed boxes of baby formula and diaper samples, magazines, baby photography offers, baby clothes, and direct-marketing flyers advertising everything from savings bonds to cord-blood banking ... The bulk of the direct mail offers, however, are for children's life insurance. I find these marketing offers particularly ghoulish. (Ebeling, 2016: 6)

Ebeling traced many of the offers back to a data broker's errant inference that she had a child. The inaccurate data had fed into numerous databases, but could not be corrected nearly as fast as it had spread (Ebeling, 2018). Typically sold at a few cents per name, lists of "moms" or "pregnant women" or any of myriad other characteristics do not need to be particularly reliable to attract eager buyers.

---

[10] Thus roughly 10 million people had errors in their credit report that could result in less favourable terms for credit.

[11] Discussing factors (like easy reproducibility and persistence) that distinguish digitized information, thereby meriting regulatory attention beyond that traditionally assigned to non-digital information.

Errant data can also result in harsh financial consequences. When it examined a large sample of consumer reports from credit bureaus in the early 2010s, the Federal Trade Commission found that at least 20 percent of them contained errors (Leibowitz et al., 2012). An important portion of these errors could substantially affect the terms of credit offered to the mischaracterized person (Leibowitz et al., 2012). As one report summarized, "Slightly more than one in 10 consumers saw a change in their credit score after the CRAs modified errors on their credit report," and "approximately one in 20 consumers had a maximum score change of more than 25 points." This amounted to over 10 million US citizens potentially denied credit, or offered worse terms, thanks to recordkeeping error. More recent scholarship has also demonstrated how scoring has exacerbated inequality (Foohey & Greene, 2021).

Underlying data sources can often be unreliable. Industrious reporters have uncovered numerous examples of persons placed on certain lists who should not be on them (such as a man curious to be placed on a list titled "diabetic interest," when he did not have the disease and had never been treated for it) (Pettypiece & Robertson, 2014a, 2014b). It's a rather remarkable story:

> Dan ... doesn't have diabetes nor is he aware of any obvious link to the disease. Try telling that to data miners. The 42-year-old information technology worker's name recently showed up in a database of millions of people with 'diabetes interest' sold by Acxiom Corp., one of the world's biggest data brokers. One buyer, data reseller Exact Data, posted [his] name and address online, along with 100 others, under the header Sample Diabetes Mailing List. It's just one of hundreds of medical databases up for sale to marketers.

The Sample Diabetes Mailing List was one of many "suffering seniors" lists. While some buyers of such lists want to advertise wares to alleviate that suffering, others want to exploit it. Thanks to the black-box nature of the industry, we have little sense of the relative balance of constructive and exploitive uses of the information.

Note, too, that I have redacted the data subject's last name, because of ongoing concerns about the indiscriminate and unlicensed use of texts (such as this very book) in generative models. Many of these models lack the ability to semantically understand a concept like negation. Therefore, the influence of a text denying the data subject's having diabetes may instead reinforce an association between the subject and diabetes, simply because the data subject's name and the word "diabetes" are in the same sentence. The inscrutable nature of many language models creates new frontiers of reputational peril, already documented in some cases of defamation by large language models (LLMs).

Nor is there much chance of finding out about such errors in the many areas of reputational scoring that are unregulated. Privacy experts Pam Dixon and Robert Gellman concluded in 2014 that, "because of lack of transparency, consumers cannot be assured of the reliability, fairness, or legality of scoring models. Inaccurate, incomplete, and illegal factors may be used today to make decisions about consumers without any oversight or redress" (Dixon & Gellman, 2014). Frustration at this untenable situation helped drive support for both the GDPR and the California privacy laws described in the following, but it is still unclear how well these initiatives will actually improve the landscape of automated generation of reputation.

2.3.2 Inappropriate Data

Even when data is accurate, it can be inappropriate for inclusion in marketing, hiring, credit, or other databases. Big data approaches, emphasizing the velocity, volume, and variety of information, along with ever-cheapening data storage costs, have encouraged firms to amass remarkable amounts of information about consumers, and to infer even more (Tufekci, 2019). Data miners, data brokers, and data resellers have created lists with highly sensitive attributes (Clifford & Silver-Greenberg, 2013; Office of Oversight and Investigations Majority Staff, 2013). Such lists and databases can then inform consumer scoring (Dixon & Gellman, 2014; Christl & Spiekermann, 2016; Christl, 2017).

The normative force of the term "inappropriate" is rooted in Helen Nissenbaum's pathbreaking work to characterize privacy as "contextual integrity" (Nissenbaum, 2004). Privacy is a multifaceted concept, but the problem of context is near its core. As Nissenbaum argues, one important source of the "normative roots of unease" at unexpected data sharing is the common ethical sense that data gathered for one purpose may be entirely inappropriate when deployed for other purposes.

Certain fiduciary relationships come with strict restrictions on data transfers (Balkin, 2016). But norms of appropriateness have far deeper moral roots than professional obligations of confidentiality. Rather, they reflect Michael Walzer's insight that certain forms of distribution are appropriate in certain spheres, and inappropriate in others (Walzer, 1983). One's degree of sickness is clearly relevant to the distribution of medical care, but not the distribution of loans or employment. To think otherwise is a step toward permitting the data economy to promote cascading disadvantages, bringing the higher risk of unemployment and bankruptcy to persons merely on account of their medical misfortunes. Such a principle of "separate spheres" of distributional justice is in deep tension with big data methods' omnivorous appetite for predictive information, revealing the profound amorality of unconstrained AI evaluation of persons.

Once data brokers assemble that information into dossiers, truly remarkable aggregations arise. As a Senate Report documented:

> Beyond publicly available information such as home addresses and phone numbers, data brokers maintain data as specific as whether consumers view a high volume of YouTube videos, the type of car they drive, ailments they may have such as depression or diabetes, whether they are a hunter, what types of pets they have; or whether they have purchased a particular shampoo product in the last six months. (Office of Oversight and Investigations Majority Staff, 2013)

Since the report was published, traces of persons' digital lives have become so common that even firms devoted to other pursuits than data aggregation can develop exceptional dossiers. For example, finance law expert Matthew Bruckner has summarized the state of play for what he calls "Version 2.0 algorithmic lenders," which

> use different inputs and a different process to evaluate prospective borrowers than traditional lenders, who typically focus primarily on a borrower's credit score. For example, [a Singapore-based firm] makes use of more than 12,000 data points gathered from social websites, such as Yahoo, Google, LinkedIn, Twitter and Facebook, to assess a consumer's potential to pay off loans. Other algorithmic lenders use different proxies for creditworthiness, such as ... online small business customer reviews ... educational history, professional licensure data, and personal property ownership data. (Bruckner, 2018: 13)

Bruckner mentions other categories of information as well, such as "a consumer's email addresses, brand of car, Facebook friends, educational background and college major, even whether he or she sends text messages in all capital letters or in lower case" (Hardy, 2012; Eveleth, 2019). Facebook also has a patent for using social media data for credit evaluation (Epstein, 2015). To be sure, such data may lead to new forms of financial inclusion. But there is little to recommend a world in which social media users feel pressure to "unfriend" or otherwise distance themselves from their more financially precarious friends, lest data in one digital realm stigmatize their reputation in another.

2.3.3 Discrimination

The digitization of judgment has long been billed as a major step toward solving discrimination. The rationale is straightforward: that a machine judging persons would be far less likely to manifest or express racial animus than a person in the same position (Woods, 2022).[12] Indeed, this assumption helped inform some of the earliest regulation of algorithmic scoring, given that the U.S. Equal Credit Opportunity Act strongly encourages the use of scores for credit underwriting purposes (Poon, 2009). There is an undeniable discipline to the quantitative expression of judgment, familiar to anyone who has graded tests with and without a numerical rubric. The hyper-complex sorting mechanisms of advanced ML are assumed to be even fairer than rubrics, as layers of feedback and tuning in neural networks may result in mechanisms even more distant from human bias than simpler score designs.

The simple story of algorithms fighting discrimination has been significantly complicated over the past decade. Dominique Williams cautions that, while "the use of this technology is believed to be a progression towards fairness, in practice, there are numerous examples of race and gender related biases resulting from the ubiquitous use of artificial intelligence technology in the decision-making process" (Williams, 2021). As law professor and sociologist Ifeoma Ajunwa has demonstrated in illuminating work on AI-driven hiring, "in some instances, automated decision-making has served to replicate and amplify bias" (Ajunwa, 2020a, 2020b, 2021).[13]

Examples of discrimination based on incomplete or biased data are myriad. Facial recognition programs have consistently misidentified or failed to identify minorities (and particularly minority women) at higher rates than for white men. As one researcher has explained, "lack of representation in datasets has created deeply rooted biases in facial recognition algorithms developed by companies and the federal government" (Fleischer, 2020). Evaluative data based on such facial recognitions could then, in turn, itself be biased – for example, by more rapidly qualifying white male residents to re-enter the country after foreign travel. Autocorrect software on phones and word processing programs "presumes Whiteness," leading it to fail to recognize "names that do not look White or Anglo" (Dyal-Chand, 2021). "Sometimes autocorrect changes names to their closest Anglo approximations (as in Ayaan to Susan)," law professor Rashmi Dyal-Chand explains, and "[s]ometimes it suggests replacements that are not proper names (as in DaShawn to dash away)." When the software of leading firms like Apple repeatedly fails at such basic versions of inclusiveness, it does not inspire confidence in more complex settings.

---

[12] Per Andrew Keane Woods (Woods, 2022: 66): "Algorithms can help fight prejudice in healthcare too. One recent study showed that algorithms spotted diseases on the x-rays of underserved populations when those same diseases were missed by doctors due to implicit bias."

[13] In the last of these (Ajunwa, 2021), Ifeoma Ajunwa develops practical disclosure remedies to address the critiques advanced in "Paradox of Automation."

Medical settings have also revealed similar problems. A health care allocation algorithm, based on spending data, systematically underallocated care to Black patients (Jee, 2019; Obermeyer et al., 2019). A tool for diagnosing Alzheimer's via voice recordings proved effective for only the Canadian dialect speakers it was trained on (Gershgorn, 2018). Reviewing such problems, law and philosophy professor Anita L. Allen has called for a "a race-conscious African American Online Equity Agenda" (Allen, 2022).

These are not isolated incidents, reflecting mere immaturity in the technology. Rather, they are a persistent risk for AI applications. As law professor Sharona Hoffman and computer scientist Andy Podgurski explain, "discrimination-related pitfalls of AI" include measurement errors, selection bias, feedback loop bias, rough heuristics, and stereotyping (Broussard, 2018; Eubanks, 2018; Benjamin, 2019; Costanza-Chock, 2020; Hoffman & Podgurski, 2020). These patterns of problematic data use and analysis have sparked critiques of AI deployments in finance, education, employment, and other contexts where the evaluation of human conduct by machines alone, or humans informed by machines, is common. In each arena, decision-makers are increasingly aware of discrimination via digitized judgments. As Joseph Blass has explained, gender impacts of the past may easily be replicated into the future, even when unintended:

> [B]ias may arise where the candidates who were granted interviews were largely–and completely by chance–men, and the candidates who were denied interviews generally–and again by chance–were women ... Such dataset artifacts can be misleading to a DLNN [deep learning neural network], and can lead to problematic discrimination down the line, depending on the function the DLNN learns. (Blass, 2019)

One commentator even raises the possibility that algorithmic decision-making may exacerbate intentional discrimination, whereby decision-makers "mask their discriminatory aims by constructing algorithms that intentionally produce discriminatory results. For example, a housing provider seeking to exclude Latinos could set its algorithm to penalize individuals in particular industries in which Latinos are disproportionately represented" (Schneider, 2020). There are numerous such proxies available, and they proliferate as data collection, swaps, and sharing advances (Terry, 2014). Scholars have demonstrated the danger of "directly discriminatory algorithms" (Adams-Prassl et al., 2023). Yet even when there is no intent to discriminate, there still are ample opportunities in AI for disparate impact by design. Sonia Katyal asks us to "Imagine ... a situation where data on job promotions might be used to predict career success, but the data was gathered from an industry that systematically promoted men instead of women" (Katyal, 2019). Given the prevalence of gender discrimination and wage gaps, such problematic data is surely widespread.

The combined documented and potential impact, of inaccurate, inappropriate, and discriminatory data, is deeply disturbing. It has led to growing calls to shine a light on the data practices at the core of our "black box society" (Pasquale, 2015). Legislation has both reinvigorated old transparency protections, and created new IARs for citizens. Section 3 explores these rights and their limits.

3 The Growth and Contested Scope of Access Rights Initiatives

As the biases of algorithmic systems are becoming clearer, experts are translating academic research and activist demands into statutes and regulations. Lawmakers are proposing bills requiring basic standards of algorithmic transparency and auditing (Biden, 2023).[14] Polities are starting down a long road toward ensuring that AI-based hiring practices and financial underwriting are not used if they have a disparate impact on historically marginalized communities.

Even enthusiasts for computational evaluations of persons now acknowledge that data can be biased, inaccurate, or inappropriate. Academics have established conferences like the ACM's "Fairness, Accountability, and Transparency" in order to create institutional forums for coders, lawyers, and social scientists to regularly interact in order to address social justice concerns (ACM Conference, n.d.). When businesses and governments announce plans to use AI, there are routine challenges and demands for audits (AI Now Institutute et al., 2018). IARs can play a pivotal role in empowering such demands, and providing important information to data subjects.

However, the proper scope of IARs is contested. To better understand why that is, this section first explores a model of how data may matter to personal evaluations like hiring dossiers and credit scoring. In Section 3.1, we revisit the hypothetical algorithmic evaluation system presented in Section 2, and explore how it might have been processing data. Section 3.2 shows how various US laws assist persons affected by such models, and Section 3.3 does the same for EU law. Section 3.4 maps some possible roads ahead for the expansion of IARs and explainability requirements, while also acknowledging stiff political opposition to them.

---

[14] See also Algorithmic Accountability Act (2019).

3.1 Modeling Algorithmic Evaluations of Persons

To explore the implications of AI in personal evaluations, consider the model for credit described at the beginning of Section 2. If Alice were to request what data was fed into the decision, and how it was processed, assume for now that she might receive any of the following responses from the firm, divided by depth of disclosure into four levels outlined in Table 1.

These levels of disclosure are neither exhaustive nor fully documented in extant firm practices, but are intended to be illustrative. They reflect a "layered approach" to disclosure (Kaminski & Malgieri, 2020).[15] As the thoroughness of disclosure increases, from levels I to IV, it goes from being more model-centric (disclosing general aspects of the model) to more subject-centric (giving the data subject more direct insights as to exactly what data was gathered about them, and how it affected the decision) (Edwards & Veale, 2017). In the example discuseed earlier, it is only at the Level IV response that Alice would discover the combination of issues that may change the outcome given the current algorithm: if the firm classifies NYTimes.com as a "serious website," then the "cleaning" of Alice's data for alleged outliers eliminated an important source of "crediting" information for her. Other problems also emerge as the explanation becomes more complete. The attribution of data points to Alice based on location alone is reminiscent of "redlining," a long-decried lending practice tending to disqualify persons from a given area, or give them worse loan terms (often on racist grounds, or with disparate racial impact), as well as its more recent version, "weblining" (which unjustly makes assumptions about persons based on the spaces they have visited online, or even where their IP address is assumed to be located) (Hernandez et al., 2001).

Given the breadth of legal and computer science literature on AI explainability, I should also stipulate further my goals for this illustrative model. Like access rights themselves, this hypothetical may be criticized both for doing too much, and too little. On the "too much" side, lenders who use simpler models may complain that such extensive use of alternative and fringe data is not yet common among algorithmic lenders. To be sure, most of the industry has been cautious about implementing highly unusual, or "fringe," data sources (Hiller & Jones, 2022). Nevertheless, there is ample precedent internationally that fringe data has been used in underwriting (Privacy International, 2017). An algorithmic lender has also sought and received a "no action" letter from the U.S. Consumer Financial Protection Bureau, indicating serious intent to deploy these

---

[15] Kaminski and Malgieri provide an academic endorsement of a "layered approach" to transparency, reminiscent of the levels of explanation above. This approach was also embraced by the European Data Protection Board (European Data Protection Board, 2022).

Table 1 Potential levels of explanation offered to the data subject

Data access request	Information about how the data was used
I. Numerous public and private records from the past year were consulted to analyze your file.	I. Machine learning was used to process your file.
II. *I above, plus*: Attached, please find a broad description of the types or records consulted (websites visited, music playlists, food purchases, and voting and arrest data) to gather data about you.	II. *I above, plus*: Five ML models processed your data. Some data points were attributed to you.
III. *II above, plus*: Detailed list of records consulted, including websites visited in the past year, which, according to our records, were [gives list of hundreds of websites]; music playlists [gives playlist titles], food purchases [gives complete list of food purchased as reflected in the firm's records], and voting and arrest data [gives title of all records consulted].	III. *II above, plus*: Some data points were attributed to you, based on characteristics of persons in our data training data set who live within 10 miles of you. Four of the models predicted you would not default or have any late payments, but one model did predict default. Our internal guidance documents do not permit offers of credit to persons classified as 1 c by any of the firm's models.
IV. *III above, plus*: Gives sources of the data, and "cleaning" processes used to eliminate outliers in Alice's record.	IV. *III above, plus*: According to some approaches we have used to interpret the model that produced the most negative prediction for your application, you have been denied credit in part because (a) you visited too many websites classed as "unserious," and did not visit "serious" websites often enough. (b) you bought too many highly processed foods. (c) you failed to vote in the last three elections. These factors were found more in groups that defaulted or paid late in our training set.

methods. The detailed questions in a multiagency request for information left little doubt that leading finance policymakers have been concerned about inexplicable AI and ML (The Treasury Department, The Comptroller of the Currency, The Federal Reserve System, The Federal Deposit Insurance Corporation, The Consumer Financial Protection Bureau, and The National Credit Union Administration, 2021). Many commentators have also indicated interest in accelerating the range of data deployed in underwriting.

On the other hand, commentators focused on what is unique about ML may complain that the model presented is too simple – that the true ML/AI difference is a form of machine "cognition" that cannot be interpreted by human beings. If the model above (or some past model) itself identified certain factors, like web browsing habits, as significant in the determination, asking how it did so may be tantamount to trying to find out what sequence of neurons activated in a loan officer's brain when they decided to grant or deny credit.

Another way to understand this admittedly daunting critique is to consider the possibility of nonlinear relationships in models. As Selbst and Barocas explain:

> A linear model is one in which there is a steady change in the value of the output as the value of the input changes. Linear models tend to be easier for humans to understand and interpret because the relationship between variables is stable and lends itself to straightforward extrapolation. In contrast, the behavior of nonlinear models can be far more difficult to predict.

One source of nonlinearity may be non-monotonicity, where "the value of the output of the model goes up and down haphazardly as the value of the input moves steadily upward" (Selbst & Barocas, 2018). For example, a non-monotonic scoring model might add 10 points to a credit score for each of the first three credit cards a person obtained, subtract 10 points for each of the next three, and add 10 points for each of the next three. There is no simple linear relationship here, and if this non-monotonicity is driven by other similarly erratic relationships, there is little hope of unraveling the relationships involved (Selbst & Barocas, 2018: 1095).

Now stipulate another layer of complexity, that reverses the sign of these effects when a borrower has lived in their primary residence for less than six months, and alters the magnitude of the point change for everyone else in an unpredictable fashion, also based on length of time lived in a primary residence. Any explanation would need to address both the number of credit cards an applicant obtained, and length of time lived in primary residence. The premise of some forms of AI and ML is that adding dozens, hundreds, or thousands more variables to the algorithm may provide similar recalibrations (and even reversals) of the impact of extant variables. One way of modeling these models, so to speak, is to think of them as finding local exceptions to general rules. For example, the general theory or rule may be that a person with a thin credit file should not be granted a loan, but ML may be able to find a subset of such persons with an interlocking set of characteristics very similar to those of successful applicants. As one journalist explains:

> The bigger the dataset, the more inconsistencies [with general rules] the AI learns. The end result is not a theory in the traditional sense of a precise claim about [a domain], but a set of claims that is subject to certain constraints. A way to picture it might be as a branching tree of 'if . . . then'-type rules, which is difficult to describe mathematically, let alone in words. (Spinney, 2022)

Given its dependence on past data sets and future prediction, such ML may ultimately be closer to historical inquiry and futurology (respectively) than natural science – but driven by computational associations far less tractable to communication than the forms of evidence more common in humanistic disciplines.[16]

The conclusion, then, for some scholars and many AI boosters, is that an "explanation" offering hundreds of decision points where some data made some presumably small impact on the borrower's score, is not useful to the borrower. Some even claim that an explanation is impossible.

There are many possible responses to this problem. For those claiming impossibility of explanation, the valence of the critique of a right to explanation can be flipped. The problem may be less with a requirement of some form of explainability, than with the use of the inexplicable model itself. While the *creation* of such models may be protected at a constitutional level in some jurisdictions by free expression guarantees, which often include a right to scientific inquiry that does not threaten imminent harm, there is no general right to use such models in regulated industries when deciding persons' opportunities. This is true even in the US, so often at the vanguard of free expression fundamentalism (Guzelian, 2008; Franks, 2019).[17] The effective prohibition of the use of models that are too complex to explain could be a predictable and laudable outcome of a robust legal requirements for explainability. It may be thought of as an industrial policy for the booming business of personal

---

[16] For important insights on the nature of statistical evidence in adjudication, as a potential form of precedent or perhaps even evidence, see Genevieve Vanderstichele, *The Normative Value of Legal Analytics. Is There a Case for Statistical Precedent?* (Vanderstichele, 2019).

[17] On potential liability for scientific speech, see Christopher P Guzelian: "nothing in established First Amendment precedent or its first principles suggests that there is a bar on liability for negligently false communications" (Guzelian, 2008). But see Mary Anne Franks on the prevalence of absolutist constructions of free speech in US jurisprudence (Franks, 2019).

evaluations, steering it toward more explainable and contestable forms. This is not an attack on algorithms *tout court*, but only on the most *avant-garde*, inexplicable ones (Pasquale & Citron, 2014).[18]

A second, less harsh response is to interpret the relevant statute as requiring only "meaningful information" about the processing of data, rather than a complete explanation of how the automated decision-making system predicted the likelihood of default, profitability, or other aspects of a relationship between the lender and the borrower. As a report on accountable automated decision-making noted, "some promising emerging research claims that thousands of features can be used while maintaining interpretability and accuracy, using new techniques to highlight only the strongest interactions between features for review" (Rieke et al., 2018). This includes research on Locally Interpretable Model-Agnostic Explanations (LIME), which may explain a model's predictions by testing how output changes given changes in key inputs, without offering a holistic account of the model as a whole (Lou et al., 2013). This is a type of explanation that may be particularly valuable to persons seeking concrete guidance as to what behaviors they might change to obtain a different result.

Selbst and Barocas have also observed that there are several aspects of such models' creation, updating, and use that can be made more transparent and accessible (Selbst & Barocas, 2018: 1130–1137). For example, to assist with model-level explanation, managers' and quality improvement specialists' communications with developers to offer feedback on existing models can be documented. Even ultra-complex LLMs might become more transparent if we had access to the full array of instructions given to workers engaged in the feedback during the "reinforcement learning by human feedback" sessions used by the firms developing the LLMs. For subject-level explanations (focused on a decision about a particular person's application), the full range of data consulted can be released.

More helpfully, firms may enable applicants to access a decision-making "sandbox" which displays the current values of key variables for the applicant and allows the applicant to test what would happen to their application if certain variables changed. For example, such an interactive application may reveal that a 5 percent rise in income or savings may greatly raise the probability of a successful application, ceteris paribus. Even when confronted by a very complex model, the applicant may be able to determine that a few changes in behavior might lead to a different outcome.

---

[18] In my 2014 article with Danielle Citron, we discuss the range of potential configurations of data and algorithm opacity and revisability.

Of course, models can change over time, and if that does occur, behavior that was deemed "crediting" at Time 1 may make no difference, or even become "discrediting," by Time 2 – particularly when variables with little intuitive relation to credit are included, like social media activity or web browsing history. However, we do not, at present, have any idea as to how commonplace such a Kafkaesque interaction with an explanation interface would be. Even if it were common, that is not necessarily an indictment of it. However frustrating it may be on an individual level to encounter a credit star chamber with constantly changing terms, this experience may spark complaints and political activism to make credit provision more responsive to public demands. Exposing volatility in such processes may be an important step toward public understanding of an AI-driven credit system.

Determining the scope of rights of access to data, or to the logic of decision-making based on personal data, raises numerous questions under overlapping legal regimes. Section 3.2 examines two dimensions of US law: relevant federal financial privacy laws, and a more comprehensive data access regime now emerging in California. Each may well result in important insights for data subjects. Section 3.3 explores data access rights in the EU context. Both sections emphasize the contested status of key dimensions of data access rights; it is by no means clear what level of access that data subjects may routinely expect. Section 3.4 examines possible futures for IARs. There are many economic arguments now being deployed to argue for narrow interpretations of access rights, which may prematurely limit the range of information available to data subjects.

3.2 Case Studies in US Rights to Information Access

There are many forms of data access rights at the federal level in the US, in contexts ranging from health care to education to finance.[19] Examining all their interactions with the digitization of judgment would take at least a book-length treatment. Section 3.2.1 narrows the federal focus to finance examples, to convey the complexity and limits of such laws in one sector. It first examines the Fair Credit Reporting Act, one of the US's oldest privacy laws, and then demonstrates how the Equal Credit Opportunity Act may create leverage for borrowers to demand an explanation of adverse actions against them, even if they are made, or merely recommended, by advanced ML systems. Section 3.2.2 offers an overview of access rights guaranteed by two California privacy statutes. These laws offer broad rights of information access to California residents, filling many of the regulatory gaps left by federal law. This is a fast-moving area, and readers should not assume that the discussions below are comprehensive portraits of the laws and

---

[19] See, for instance, Health Insurance Portability and Accountability Act; Family Educational Right to Privacy Act; Children's Online Privacy Protection Act.

regulations discussed. Rather, they are intended to document the types of controversies that have arisen as judges, regulators, and legislators try to clarify the scope of rights to data access and AI explainability.

3.2.1 Fair Credit Reporting Act and Equal Credit Opportunity Act

Under US law, a data subject may exercise their rights under the Fair Credit Reporting Act (2018), which offers broad guarantees of rights of access to credit reports (Havard, 2011; Lauer, 2017). However, FCRA is a narrowly crafted law. It was designed for a tripartite structure of information exchange: creditors sending either positive or derogatory information about consumers to credit bureaus, which in turn compile this (and other) data into reports to be shared with clients.[20] In the Act's parlance, "furnishers" provide data to "consumer reporting agencies" (CRAs), which compile this data and present it to users.[21] Focusing regulation on this particular set of information exchanges left several loopholes for secret data to enter borrower evaluation processes.

For example, a credit card company deciding to raise or reduce an existing customer's credit limit on the basis of items purchased using the card is not a CRA, since it is using its own data. Even very intimate data may drive such determinations. Given strict trade secrecy protections, such applications of data-driven classification are rarely discovered. Nevertheless, their very possibility reveals a gaping hole at the heart of the FCRA regime: the ability of financial firms to compile their own data sets on customers, not subject to the strictures imposed when such information-gathering is outsourced.

While bank-affiliated lenders are regulated under FCRA, direct lenders (which make loans directly to consumers, avoiding any interactions with third-parties) are not (Bruckner, 2018). The rise of direct lending fintechs, making underwriting decisions based in part on information that is not specifically compiled for credit evaluation purposes, fundamentally challenges the premises of FCRA. It also undermines efforts to ensure that data is evaluated in context, since "big data" methods tend to strip down classifiers and evaluations into acontextualized numerical values. Maintaining context is an important ethical value in data protection law (Nissenbaum, 2004). As algorithmic lenders grow,

---

[20] See 12 C.F.R § 1022.41, noting that "furnisher means an entity that furnishes information relating to consumers to one or more consumer reporting agencies for inclusion in a consumer report."

[21] See 15 U.S.C. § 1681a (2018) ("The term 'consumer reporting agency' means any person which, for monetary fees, dues, or on a cooperative nonprofit basis, regularly engages in whole or in part in the practice of assembling or evaluating consumer credit information or other information on consumers for the purpose of furnishing consumer reports to third parties, and which uses any means or facility of interstate commerce for the purpose of preparing or furnishing consumer reports").

consumer rights under FCRA will decline in importance. Even when a CRA is involved, banks may use data to transform an existing CRA's score (by, e.g., multiplying a reported score by a coefficient based on their own data), and FCRA responsibilities may not attach to this step of the process. As two US scholars have observed:

> Whether a particular entity or reporting activity falls under FCRA principally depends on the types of information involved, the actual or expected uses of that information, and whether the information is reported by a consumer reporting agency ... For example, a lender that develops its own mechanisms for collection and data analytics will not trigger FCRA as long as it does not resell that information for further use in the credit, insurance, or employment context. (Hurley & Adebayo, 2016: 185, 187)

Had the algorithmic lender in our hypothetical received a credit report from a consumer reporting agency, it would have needed to give Alice a "notice of adverse action" under FCRA.[22] Such a notice gives a consumer the right to obtain the information relied on for the adverse action. This includes the disclosure of a credit score if it was relied upon. As a Federal Reserve Bank examiner has explained, "not only the score, but also the range of possible credit scores; all the key factors that adversely affected the credit score; the date on which the credit score was created; and the name of the person or entity providing the credit score or the information upon which score was created, must be provided" (Ammermann, 2013). If Alice were to request an algorithmic lender release to her the data used to make its decision, it would likely simply respond that it is a "direct lender," unconstrained by the FCRA (Hurley & Adebayo, 2016).

An attempt to apply FCRA to Google exposes just how limited FCRA's reach is. In *Sandofsky v. Google LLC* (2021), an attorney proceeding pro se argued that "employers, landlords, and others use the Google search engine to find data" on himself, and on a putative class of individual consumers, "for the purpose of evaluating whether to transact business with them, employ them, or associate with them generally" (*Sandofsky v Google*: 1). Sandofsky believed that Google was essentially acting as a CRA, merely automating its consumer reports as search results rather than dispensing them in more traditional formats. The FCRA defines a "consumer reporting agency" as

---

[22] See 15 U.S.C. § 1681m(h) ("If any person takes any adverse action § 615–15 U.S.C. § 1681m71 with respect to any consumer that is based in whole or in part on any information contained in a consumer report, the person shall (1) provide oral, written, or electronic notice of the adverse action to the consumer; and (2) provide to the consumer written or electronic disclosure (A) of a numerical credit score as defined in section 609(f)(2) (A) used by such person in taking any adverse action based in whole or in part on any information in a consumer report").

[A]ny person, which, for monetary fees, dues, or on a cooperative nonprofit basis, regularly engages in whole or in part in the practice of assembling or evaluating consumer credit information or other information on consumers for the purpose of furnishing consumer reports to third parties. 15 U.S.C. § 1681a. (f)

The court in *Sandofsky* refused to characterize Google as "assembling or evaluating consumer credit information or other information on consumers" when it compiles name search results (*Sandofsky v Google*: 3). It claimed that to assemble or evaluate, in this context, involves "more than receipt and retransmission of information" (*Sandofsky v Google*: 5).[23] Sandofsky did no better on the other prongs of the definition. The court looked back to a 1990 guidance from the FTC, which stated that "a publisher of public information" does not become a consumer reporting agency simply because of "possible use" of its products "for consumer purposes by a few subscribers" (*Sandofsky v Google*: 5).[24]

Given the law's narrow definition of CRAs, there are many opportunities for financial firms to avoid FCRA strictures as well. However, even direct lenders (as well as those engaging with CRAs) are covered by the Equal Credit Opportunity Act of 1976 and its implementing Regulation B. These legal authorities impose certain adverse action notice requirements to creditors, regardless of how they obtained their information about applicants.[25] These duties of explanation are premised on ECOA's anti-discrimination mission. ECOA prohibits discrimination against borrowers and applicants for credit "on the basis of race, color, religion, national origin, sex or marital status, or age (provided the applicant has the capacity to contract)" (15 U.S.C. § 1691(a)(1)). To promote enforcement of its antidiscrimination rules, ECOA requires certain disclosures in adverse action notices. These include a "statement of the action taken by the creditor," and either "a statement of the specific reasons for the action taken," or a "disclosure of the applicant's right to a statement of specific reasons and the name, address, and telephone number of the person or office from which this information can be obtained" (Ammermann, 2013). Regulation B goes on to require that "statement of reasons ... must be specific and indicate the principal reason(s) for the adverse action" (12 C.F.R. § 202.9(b)(2)).

---

[23] Citing *Smith v. First Nat'l Bank of Atlanta* (1988) (quoting *D'Angelo v. Wilmington Med. Ctr., Inc* (1981)).

[24] Citing Commentary on the Fair Credit Reporting Act (1990).

[25] Under the ECOA, an adverse action includes any "refusal to grant credit in substantially the amount or on substantially the terms requested in an application unless the creditor makes a counteroffer (to grant credit in a different amount or on other terms), and the applicant uses or expressly accepts the credit offered."

The Consumer Financial Protection Bureau (CFPB) (which shares authority to enforce both FCRA and ECOA with other agencies) has published model adverse action notice forms, which largely focus on traditional rationales for adverse action (Consumer Financial Protection Bureau, n.d.).[26] For example, the lender using the form could check "collection action or judgment," "garnishment or attachment," "foreclosure or repossession," among about twenty other rationales. The standard form would, of course, be less useful for an algorithmic than a traditional lender, since the types of information likely determinative of the decision are either distinct from traditional credit data, or may not be subject to brief explanation.

To help fill this vacuum, the Federal Trade Commission has offered guidance on Regulation B and ECOA as well.[27] The agency has advised businesses to explain decisions based on AI, just as they would handle older and simpler models:

> If you deny consumers something of value based on algorithmic decision-making, explain why . . . [I]t's not good enough simply to say 'your score was too low' or 'you don't meet our criteria.' You need to be specific (e.g., 'you've been delinquent on your credit obligations' or 'you have an insufficient number of credit references'). This means that you must know what data is used in your model and how that data is used to arrive at a decision. And you must be able to explain that to the consumer. If you are using AI to make decisions about consumers in any context, consider how you would explain your decision to your customer if asked. (Smith, 2020)

In response to such guidance, several firms have sought further clarification of Regulation B's disclosure requirements.

There have been spirited debates about the feasibility of explanations in varied algorithmic contexts. Some scholars have expressed doubts about the possibility of complete, satisfying, or even helpful explanations. Others have tried to meet their concerns, or to propose iterative methods of testing models that reveal how they respond to certain changes in inputs, even if they do not accomplish a deep explanation of the relationships between key variables. If policymakers assume an ex post approach to the problem, and conceive of their

---

[26] The CFPB shares authority here with other financial regulators, but the Dodd-Frank Act has made clear that, when the agency is interpreting FCRA and ECOA, courts owe it the deference due to agencies which have sole authority over implementing a statute.

[27] The FTC also has authority to interpret and enforce these laws. FTC Staff Comment to the CFPB Regarding Regulation B and ECOA, available at (Division of Financial Practices, 2021) ("Under the Act, the FTC retained its authority to enforce ECOA and Regulation B. In addition, the Act gave the Commission the authority to enforce any CFPB rules applicable to entities within the FTC's jurisdiction, which include most providers of financial services that are not banks, thrifts, or federal credit unions").

role as merely regulating finished products after they have been developed, the resolution (or at least refinement) of such academic debates will be of decisive importance to the future of AI explainability in personal evaluations.

However, another conception of AI explainability – as ex ante industrial policy, as opposed to ex post regulation, may be valuable here. Government may decide that, regardless of the sacrifice to profit it may bring, personal evaluations should meet some baseline of explainability. Such evaluations are not predefined products, but rather are services and processes, which can be altered to reflect public values. By requiring certain levels of explainability, government can effectively shift some investment away from mere profit maximization and toward the promotion of intelligibility.

Admittedly, if the demands for explainability become too burdensome, certain forms of technological advance in prediction may be foreclosed. However, the realm of personal evaluation has always been, and should continue to be, quasi-juridical in nature, and therefore subject to public values, including baseline levels of transparency. Moreover, it is important not to overestimate the potential value of AI methods to predict whether an applicant will be, say, a good credit risk, a diligent student, or a responsible employee. Such technologies of evaluation may threaten important social values. For example, we may someday find out that analyzing behavior in kindergarten leads to a 3 percent increase in accuracy for colleges looking to admit high-earning students or employers looking to hire employees who will stay at least three years at their firm. Even if we were to concede that these were the right goals for the algorithm, adding in such behavioral data would violate core principles of autonomy and justice. Adults should not be judged for their behavior in childhood, because this behavior occurred before they can be expected to have developed a full sense of moral responsibility. Many other uses of decontextualized data may also be objected to on the basis of related, if less forceful, grounds.

3.2.2 California Consumer Privacy Act and California Privacy Rights Act

FCRA and ECOA are two of many federal laws offering access rights to information on a narrow, sectoral basis. Drafted to solve particular problems posed by entities like credit bureaus and lenders, these laws are subject to varied forms of regulatory arbitrage. The result has been decried by some scholars as a privacy wild west, where an extraordinary range of intimate personal data is traded without the awareness of data subjects (Rostow, 2017; Olmstead, 2021).[28]

---

[28] See Molly Olmstead (Olmstead, 2021) describing how the private data was likely purchased.

States have begun to step into this breach, adding to sectoral protections and, in at least one case, offering omnibus privacy rules. The California Consumer Privacy Act (CCPA) gave broad rights to California citizens, including "the right to know, through a general privacy policy and with more specifics available upon request, what personal information a business has collected about them, where it was sourced from, what it is being used for, whether it is being disclosed or sold, and to whom it is being disclosed or sold" (Hartzog & Richards, 2020).[29] The CPRA (passed by ballot initiative) went into effect in January, 2023, expanding consumer rights of access (and the motivation to use them) (Monticollo et al., 2020). The CPRA's text requires special attention to "sensitive information," and gives consumer rights to stop its use and sharing (Cal Civ. Code: § 1798.121).

Some of the CCPA's beneficiaries have been surprised by the dossiers they have received. For example, after receiving a "right to know" request from reporter Kari Paul, Amazon sent her "two Excel spreadsheets, more than 20,000 lines each, with titles, time stamps and actions detailing [her] reading habits on the Kindle app on [her] iPhone," among many other records. As she explained:

> I now know that on 15 February 2019 starting at 4.37pm, I read *The Deeper the Water the Uglier the Fish* – a dark novel by Katya Apekina – for 20 minutes and 30 seconds. On 5 January 2019 starting at 6.27pm, I read the apocalypse-thriller *Severance* by Ling Ma for 31 minutes and 40 seconds. Starting at 2.12pm on 3 November 2018, I read mermaid romance tale *The Pisces* by Melissa Broder for 20 minutes and 24 seconds. (Paul K., 2020: 1)

It is not hard to see how such time stamps may be the basis of more intimate inferences. For example, a person who frequently reads between two and four in the morning might be tagged as a possible insomniac. The spreadsheet included other data about her; for example, how often she looked up words and how long she lingered on a page. At least one firm – Fandango – has been reporting inferences, too. It not only told one reporter what his movie viewing history was but also that Fandango believes he likes the Muppets (which was indeed true) (Fowler, 2020).

Admittedly, my discussion, like many other academic accounts, already tends toward overreliance on innocuous information and journalistic accounts of IARs. But this is to be expected in discussions of data protection. Few, if any, persons are likely to publicly share the revelation of sensitive information they are deeply embarrassed about. This is yet another dimension of the "black box" problem in privacy policy.

---

[29] Citing (Mathews & Bowman, 2018).

Journalists are also testing the bounds of the CCPA right to know. For example, *Washington Post* reporter Geoffrey Fowler sent a request to Amazon for his data, but it did not include the data the massive retailer "collects in its camera-equipped Amazon Go convenience stores" (Fowler, 2020). Fowler then asked for a video of himself that had been collected by the retailer. This type of poking and prodding at the practical limits of IARs is a cornerstone of algorithmic accountability movements. Empiricists in the academy are often frustrated by the "black box" nature of algorithmic decision-making; they can work with legal scholars and activists to open up certain aspects of it (via freedom of information requests and application of laws guaranteeing fair data practices). Journalists have been teaming up with computer programmers and social scientists to expose new privacy-violating technologies of data collection, analysis, and use – and to push regulators to crack down on the worst offenders.

Researchers are going beyond the analysis of extant data, and joining coalitions of watchdogs, archivists, open data activists, and public interest attorneys, to assure a more balanced set of "raw materials" for analysis, synthesis, and critique. Social scientists and others must commit to the vital, long-term project of assuring that algorithms are producing fair and relevant documentation; otherwise, states, banks, insurance companies, and other powerful actors will make and own more and more inaccessible data about society and people. Algorithmic accountability is a big tent project, requiring the skills of theorists and practitioners, lawyers, social scientists, journalists, and others.

Such coordinated action will also be crucial as other layers of data disclosure are demanded over time. Many corporate inferences and evaluations will be important to consumers trying to understand the full story of how their digital personae are being processed and understood in commerce. For example, given scandals about Facebook employees who spied on the email or messaging accounts of persons they knew or were interested in, a consumer may want to know if there were unusual aspects of access to their data within the firm holding it.[30] However, early evidence suggests that firms are not providing such information, as it has not appeared in public accounts of categories of information granted pursuant to CCPA requests. This is one way in which access rights under California law are relatively ambiguous and can lead to multiple interpretations of the level of disclosure required.

The boundaries of the right of access were also the subject of comments to California's Consumer Privacy Protection Agency (CPPA) during an early rulemaking process. The comments came in response to a rulemaking begun by the

---

[30] Gloria Moralidad and Ameya Palej provide accounts of this type of inappropriate snooping (Moralidad, 2021; Paleja, 2021). There are potential criminal penalties for such snooping in the health care context. 42 U.S.C § 1320d-6.

Agency to clarify several aspects of the law. The CCPA had ordered the California Attorney General to consider disclosure of "meaningful information about the logic involved in [automated] decision-making processes" concerning the requesting consumer.[31] This would directly motivate something like the Levels III and IV disclosures mentioned in the consumer finance hypothetical depicted in the chart in Figure 1 (Pardau, 2018).[32] The CPRA shifted decision-making responsibility to the California Privacy Protection Agency, which has asked for public comments on many questions, including the following: "What information businesses must provide to consumers in response to access requests, including what businesses must do in order to provide 'meaningful information about the logic' involved in the automated decision-making process" (California Privacy Protection Agency, 2021).[33]

Firms commenting in response were quick to advocate for minimal interpretations of access rights. For example, one financial firm advocated for a 'privacy notice [outlining] what types of data are used in AI/ML models.' "(Rocket Mortgage, 2021: 181)." The firm complained that "meaningful information to a consumer about the logic is unduly burdensome to require a company to track, personalize, and provide" (Rocket Mortgage, 2021: 182).

---

[31] Cal. Civ. Code § 1798.185a, a(16) (2022).

[32] It is at present unclear to what extent federal law may preempt California law here. To avoid preemption concerns, the CCPA "excludes certain personal information covered by [some] federal privacy laws." The CCPA explicitly states that its provisions do not apply to information "bearing on a consumer's credit worthiness, credit standing, credit capacity, character, general reputation, personal characteristics, or mode of living by a consumer reporting agency" to the extent the regulated entity "is subject to regulation under the Fair Credit Reporting Act, Section 1681 et seq., Title 15 of the United States Code and the information is not used, communicated, disclosed, or sold except as authorized by the Fair Credit Reporting Act." CAL. CIV. CODE § 1798.175 (West 2022). Therefore, CCPA stands poised to fill some of the regulatory gaps identified in Section III.A.1. above, but would not apply to consumer reporting agencies or transactions solely based on information they provide. Helen Goster & Maayan Lattin, Exempt or not exempt? Part 2: The California Consumer Privacy Act and the Fair Credit Reporting Act, Practitioner Insights Commentaries (2019 WL 2261129) ("discussing the extent to which the CCPA will exempt personal information from consumer reports that are already subject to the requirements of the Fair Credit Reporting Act"). ECOA does not pose major preemption concerns regarding requirements for explainability because it does not preempt "the laws of any State with respect to credit discrimination, except to the extent that those laws are inconsistent with any provision of this subchapter, and then only to the extent of the inconsistency." 15 U.S.C. § 1691d (f) (2022). Regulation B includes similar language, and specifies that a state law that is more protective of an applicant would not be considered inconsistent. 12 C.F.R. § 202.11 (a) (2022).

[33] See the California Privacy Protection Agency (California Privacy Protection Agency, 2021: 3) citing Cal. Civil Code, § 1798.185(a)(16), "Issuing regulations governing access and opt-out rights with respect to businesses' use of automated decision-making technology, including profiling and requiring businesses' response to access requests to include meaningful information about the logic involved in those decision-making processes, as well as a description of the likely outcome of the process with respect to the consumer."

Businesses are not alone in expressing their concerns about the burdens and limits of IARs. Some researchers have also worried that even engineers cannot understand the workings of complex models. Others have claimed that consumers may not be competent to use information they obtain to better navigate automated decision-making systems. While substantial, these concerns can be addressed. Explainability is not a simple binary. Sometimes, simply learning that a particular type of data, or particularly inaccurate source of data, has been used in a decision, may be enough to taint the decision in the public eye, and even to trigger litigation. For instance, a hiring algorithm that secretly used medical records of any kind would raise serious concerns (Hoffman, 2018; Hoffman & Podgurski, 2020).[34] One does not need to understand much about how such data is used, in order to object to its use, based on a Walzer-ian principle of the impropriety of transferring data from one sphere to another when the former is inappropriate in the latter. Think, for instance, of elementary school records being used for a promotion decision for a forty-year-old, or podiatric records being used to determine if someone should be entitled to lease an apartment. There are also methods of making generally opaque ML models "locally interpretable," to understand the effect of certain shifts in weights of different variables on the predictions of the algorithm (Mittelstadt et al., 2019).

Given these demonstrable benefits of robust IARs, the Center for Democracy and Technology (an NGO) has promoted transparency as a way to "guard against algorithmic bias" (Center for Democracy and Technology, 2021: 24). Unlike the bare-bones disclosure standards urged by some businesses in comments, CDT argued a right to know "include[s] information necessary for consumers to understand the decision that was made and how it was made. At minimum, the right to access should include the principal reasons for adverse actions, specific data used in the decision, and how the system arrived at its output" (Center for Democracy and Technology, 2021: 25). This formulation could lead to more details than contemplated at Level IV of the chart in the hypothetical explored at the beginning of this section (and introduced in Section 2), since it would presumably require a further narrative or causal account of the effects of variables (or groups of variables) where Alice's dossier most significantly deviated from the median or average data points for parallel values in the training set (Tilly, 2006; Marcus & Davis, 2019; Pearl & Mackenzie, 2019).[35] Such revelations would also be an important step toward

---

[34] Sharona Hoffman argues that algorithmic discrimination may violate Title VI of the Civil Rights Act (Hoffman, 2018).

[35] Charles Tilley provides a comparison of different forms of explanation (Tilly, 2006). For a positive case for the importance of causal explanation in machine learning, see Judea Pearl and Dana Mackenzie (Pearl & Mackenzie, 2019). Though neural networks inspired by the molecular structure of the brain have accomplished much in recent years, there is still a great deal of doubt over whether they can actually reason. This doubt has led to some revival of interest

assuring trustworthy research on consumer behavior at firms, that is properly documented and not violative of privacy laws (Richards & Hartzog, 2017).

The Electronic Frontier Foundation (EFF) and American Civil Liberties Union (ACLU) have taken a similarly broad approach (EFF and ACLU, 2021: 169). They argue that "businesses should still be prepared to answer some simple questions, such as what factors were used in the decision, how those factors were weighted to reach that decision, and the confidence with which the system made that decision" (EFF and ACLU, 2021: 170). Complexity may make a report of such weightings difficult, but, by the same token, digital documentation means that files may be swiftly transferred to consumers, or to trusted third parties they delegate to help them try to understand the relevant data. Consumers may call upon civil society groups or academics to help them make sense of particularly lengthy disclosures.[36] The EFF and ACLU further argue that "where the data that feeds a profile is determined through automated decision-making, consumers should be able to obtain information that allows them to understand how those decisions were made" (EFF and ACLU, 2021: 171). Another NGO, Consumer Reports, believes that all identifiable data should be released to the consumer in response to a request (Consumer Reports, 2021: 66).

Given the ambiguity of the relevant statutes, the wide range of comments on access rights and rights to meaningful information about information processing help demonstrate the broad scope of possible outcomes for the clarification of such rights in California. Many firms have already complied with CPPA rules on information access, but giving meaningful information about data processing will demand more resources. Meanwhile, while some states have introduced new privacy laws to address the digital economy, and many others are considering them, the general status of IARs in the US is a checkered patchwork of sectoral federal and varying state laws. Europe offers a distinctive and more unified approach, but as we shall see, its protections are also ambiguous in important ways.

3.3 The European Approach to Rights to Information Access

There is much to learn from Europe about how to guarantee citizens meaningful information about the digital processes used to evaluate them. For example, France provided for such rights in the 1970s (Naudts et al., 2022). By 1995, the EU as a whole adopted a Data Protection Directive (DPD), instructing all

---

in more symbolic (and, hopefully, more explainable) approaches. As an example, see, for example, Gary Marcus's *Rebooting AI* (Marcus & Davis, 2019).

[36] For examples of citizen/NGO collaboration, see Section 4.

member states to enact laws guaranteeing their citizens rights of access to data about them held by many entities, including the corporations that are the focus of this Element (Church et al., 1999).[37] The DPD also gave EU citizens a right to demand meaningful information about automated decision-making they were subject to (Hildebrandt, 2012).

As problematic examples of the digitization of judgment multiplied, there was growing consensus among EU data protection experts and European Commission staffers on the need to update existing data protections and to apply them directly (rather than through the mediation of member state laws required by a mere directive). This effort culminated in the adoption of the GDPR.[38] As one expert on European privacy regulation, Margot Kaminski, has summarized, "The GDPR establishes a system of generally applicable notification and access rights" (Kaminski, 2019a). The GDPR has established a particularly robust set of disclosure rights for consumers, with concomitant potential for Data Protection Authorities (DPAs) of member states to inspect the data practices of firms.

3.3.1 Rights Triggered by the Collection of Data

The GDPR governs "personal data," defined as "any information relating to an identified or identifiable natural person ('data subject')" (GDPR art 4(1)). Article 15 of the GDPR guarantees a "right of access [to personal data] by the data subject" (GDPR art 15(1)), which includes multiple specific guarantees. Not only the data itself, but also its source, the purposes of its processing, and its ultimate destination and use are to be provided (GDPR art 15(1)). Thus Article 15 is designed to provide to data subjects expansive rights of access.

Articles 13 and 14 establish correlative duties for data controllers. Under Article 13 of the GDPR, when a data controller collects data from a data subject, it must also provide a wide range of information to the data subject about the purposes of the data collection, and how long the data will be stored (or the criteria used to determine that storage period) (GDPR art 13(1)(c)). It must also provide notice of certain rights of the data subject, including the right to withdraw consent for the data collection, and the right to lodge a complaint

---

[37] As Church et al. state, "[T]he individual is granted a right of access to personal information held by another party, and the individual must be able to exercise that right without excessive delay or expense" (Church et al., 1999).
[38] *Regulation (EU) 2016/679 of the European Parliament and of the Council of 27 April 2016 on the Protection of Natural Persons with Regard to the Processing of Personal Data and on the Free Movement of Such Data, and Repealing Directive 95/46/EC (General Data Protection Regulation)* [2016] OJ L 119. [Hereinafter GDPR].

with a supervisory authority (GDPR art 21: right to withdraw consent; art 77: right to lodge complaint).

Article 14 covers situations where personal data have not been provided directly by the data subject. The obligations are similar to those specified in Article 13, including notifying the data subject of any new purposes the data will be used for beyond those already disclosed by the original collector. Helena Vrabec offers one of many examples of the importance of such a notice:

> Most people who share personal data on social media expect it to be processed for the purpose of enabling online communication and find it surprising when this data is processed as part of a recruitment strategy. Without receiving specific, preliminary information about intended purposes, it is extremely difficult for any individual to ascertain how specific data is actually being used. Conveying information about the purposes is even more important as data reuse is increasingly carried out behind the scenes. (Uršič, 2021: 74)

Notifications here serve an educative function for the data subject, though they may themselves become burdensome over time if repeated across multiple interactions (Calo, 2012; Doerr et al., 2016).[39] Much work remains to be done to develop systems of records and notices that provide meaningful and useful information without annoying repetition or excessive complexity.

There are some exceptions and limitations which diminish the force of Article 14 protections. For example, where the provision of such information "proves impossible or would involve a disproportionate effort, in particular for processing for archiving purposes in the public interest, scientific or historical research purposes or statistical purposes," the GDPR does not command it (see GDPR art 14(5)(b)). As with the enforcement of many other rights, this proportionality requirement may significantly limit the range of information that data and model subjects may demand from data controllers and processors (see GDPR art 14(5)(b)). And as at least one recital relevant to Article 14 suggests, there is much to be specified regarding the exact form of the required disclosures. Complainants have already disputed the right of access compliance by firms such as streaming services and social media companies (Mahieu & Ausloos, 2020).

The questions of impossibility and disproportionate effort are of great interest for the future of access rights, putting their scope into question. A firm may either sincerely or opportunistically claim that Levels II, III, or

---

[39] This has been documented with respect to the "cookie notice fatigue" problem, and remains to be solved by policymakers. There is ongoing work in human-computer interaction to devise forms of notice that are less burdensome. See in (Calo, 2012) promoting "visceral notice" as one of many ways to improve notice practices.

IV of disclosure in the diagram in Section 3.1 are excessively burdensome. An unscrupulous firm (or one simply trying to reduce data retention costs) could take advantage of the "impossibility" exception by programming systems to delete the data used to make inferences, and then the inferences themselves, some period of time after a decision has been made. That deletion would make it impossible to discover the data. This possibility demonstrates one divergence between data protection and privacy values. Whereas the deletion may be a boon to data subjects' privacy (indeed, the GDPR itself requires the establishment of standard retention periods), it could also undermine both data subject and societal interests in data preservation. Access requests may also be frustrated without any intentional effort by firms to foil them. Firms have already asserted that they are essentially "too big to comply" with many data access requests (Ausloos, 2018; Boniface et al., 2019).[40] To what extent will they be required to redesign data retention systems in order to accommodate IARs?

This will be an ongoing topic of contestation as the GDPR is applied. Its resolution may in part depend on the interpretation of proportionality limits on access rights. DPAs and courts will gradually define the level of expense and effort deemed "disproportionate" to the benefits expected from specific access requests. Will this lead to a general jurisprudence of how much of firm revenue is expected to be expended with respect to particular duties of data protection? That would seem to be one way of defining the concept of proportionality to protect smaller firms, which some commentators believe have been disadvantaged by the GDPR (Layton, 2019). However, proportionality analysis should also address the full range of social benefits arising out of disclosure – the main topic of Section 4.

3.3.2 Rights Triggered by the Automated Processing of Data

A particular type of data analysis – profiling – triggers other rights under the GDPR. Profiling includes "any form of automated processing of personal data consisting of the use of personal data to evaluate certain personal aspects relating to a natural person, in particular to analyze or predict aspects concerning that natural person's performance at work, economic situation, health, personal preferences, interests, reliability, behavior, location or movements"

---

[40] See also per Ausloos: "essentially, Facebook's argument comes down to (a) yes, we do retain all this data; (b) we use it for 'data analytics'; but (c) we can't give you access (and as a consequence also can't erase) your personal data on a granular level. Why? Because we designed our systems in such a way that we do not have the capacity to accommodate your requests at scale ... Unfortunately, Facebook's 'too big to comply' argument is not an exception" (Ausloos, 2018).

(GDPR art 4(4)).[41] When automated processing occurs, Article 22 of the GDPR gives persons "the right not to be subject to a decision based solely on automated processing," with three exceptions, such as when consent is given by the data subject, or when a member state explicitly exempts particularly types of profiling from Article 22.

Whether or not the exceptions apply, companies regulated pursuant to the GDPR still must give the data subjects they profile "at least the right to obtain human intervention on the part of the controller, to express his or her point of view and to contest the decision" (GDPR art 22(3)). As Margot Kaminski has observed, parallel provisions in Articles 13, 14, and 15 mandate the provision of "meaningful information about the logic involved" in automated processing, "as well as the significance and the envisaged consequences of such processing for the data subject" (Selbst & Powles, 2017; Kaminski, 2019b).[42] This amounts to a right to understand the data processing involved, and its possible effects (European Commission, 2017; Malgieri & Comandé, 2017).

Recitals in the preamble of the GDPR clarify the scope of rights attendant to Article 22.[43] Yet the broad scope of the GDPR and the pervasiveness of automated decision-making have created numerous ambiguities about the law's application. How "deep" of an explanation will be required? To what extent will it be limited by trade secrecy protections asserted by firms? These are open questions at the moment, clouding the future of the right to an explanation.

Skeptics of the right to an explanation have also offered several rationales for why it will fail to play an important role in data protection in the future. Article 22 only applies to decisions made "solely" by automated processing, so firms may try to evade its strictures by introducing a person to do a brief and cursory review of what the machine recommends (Wachter et al., 2017). Judges and data policymakers in Europe will need to draw careful lines around what actually counts as human review, to keep this exception from swallowing the rule. There are also concerns that advanced ML processes may be too complex to be

---

[41] See also GDPR art 4(2): "'processing' means any operation or set of operations which is performed on personal data or on sets of personal data, whether or not by automated means, such as collection, recording, organisation, structuring, storage, adaptation or alteration, retrieval, consultation, use, disclosure by transmission, dissemination or otherwise making available, alignment or combination, restriction, erasure or destruction."

[42] See (Kaminski, 2019b) citing Articles. 13(2)(f), 14(2)(g), 15(1)(h). See in (Selbst & Powles, 2017) explaining that "Articles 13 and 14 are notification duties imposed on data controllers and Article 15 provides a right to access information throughout processing."

[43] As explained in (Kaminski, 2019b), "The GDPR consists of both text (Articles) and an extensive explanatory preamble. The preambular provisions, known as Recitals, do not have the direct force of law in the EU. A Recital is supposed to 'cast light on the interpretation to be given to a legal rule [but] it cannot in itself constitute such a rule'. This gives Recitals a liminal legal status– they are not binding law, but they are often cited as authoritative interpretations where the GDPR is vague."

usefully or meaningfully explained to consumers (Edwards & Veale, 2017). However, there are always basic questions and features of the ML process that may be interrogated and exposed, as the four-level model of explanation described earlier demonstrates. Even if algorithms at the heart of certain forms of ML transcend all human understanding, it is possible to inspect the data that are fed into them.

Critics of the right have often begun with discussions of the problems posed by complex ML algorithms for any accessible explanation. Proponents have rightly countered with the growing importance of explainable AI, particularly in fields where it is deployed to assign benefits and burdens to persons. Too often lost in the discussion has been the humble (and powerful) origins of the right of explanation in prior rights to access the data used in profiling. The more one consults industry-standard guidebooks on the creation of profiling models, the more apparent it becomes that the "right of explanation," far from being an exotic or untoward demand on the time and resources of ML designers, has instead initiated valuable reflections on the degree of context needed to make data gathering understandable to a data subject. For example, the step-by-step discussion of model-building in Naeem Siddiqi's *Intelligent Credit Scoring* suggests numerous points of inquiry, ranging from extrapolated inferences, poor quality or missing data, cherry-picked variables, changes in organizational direction or priorities, and whether scoring was done in-house or outsourced (Siddiqi, 2016).

Ongoing clarifications of the bounds of access rights, from data to profiling, will proceed in a granular fashion, based on guidance from particular disputes. Commentary from three European data law experts on a decision giving Ola drivers' access to meaningful information about the algorithms evaluating them illuminates the stakes:

> In the Ola case, for the first time, a Court require[d] an organization to explain the logic behind a fully automated decision in the sense of the GDPR. Many scholars (including us) thought that the GDPR provisions on automated decision-making and a right to an explanation would remain a dead letter ... However, this recent Ola judgment shows that Courts can actually apply these GDPR provisions in practice. Hence ... organizations that use fully automated decision-making that seriously affects people must be able to explain the logic behind such decisions. (Gellert et al., 2021)

The Worker Info Exchange has celebrated a victory in an Amsterdam appellate court giving it rights of access that would trump platform employers' assertions of trade secrecy (Worker Info Exchange, 2023). However, the victory was of limited value because of the court's focus on empowering workers to correct incorrect data, and to find data in violation of the law (Dubal, 2024).

Future member-state court decisions will further clarify the scope of obligations attendant on fully automated decision-making.[44] When proportionality concerns arise, courts and relevant regulatory bodies may turn to review the actual effects of IARs on individuals and businesses (just as the CCPA is now reviewing comments on the consequences of IARs). Section 3.4 describes the rise of an increasingly economistic discourse on these consequences.

3.4 Ongoing Uncertainty about and Backlash against IARs

The access rights described previously create several opportunities and dilemmas for privacy policymakers. In addition to the uncertainties canvassed earlier, there are ongoing forward-looking requests for comment. For example, an important multiagency request for information honed in on information access issues raised by the Equal Credit Opportunity Act:

> [ECOA] requires creditors to notify an applicant of the principal reasons for taking adverse action for credit or to provide an applicant a disclosure of the right to request those reasons. What approaches can be used to identify the reasons for taking adverse action on a credit application, when AI is employed? Does Regulation B provide sufficient clarity for the statement of reasons for adverse action when AI is used? If not, please describe in detail any opportunities for clarity. (The Treasury Department, The Comptroller of the Currency, The Federal Reserve System, The Federal Deposit Insurance Corporation, The Consumer Financial Protection Bureau, and The National Credit Union Administration, 2021)

Similarly, the California Privacy Protection Agency and European member states' Data Protection Authorities face myriad decision points as they specify the breadth and scope of information rights.

Decisions that will determine the future scope of IARs are now being made amidst a burgeoning backlash against privacy regulation. Robust access rights increase the regulatory burden of data protection laws on businesses. Some commentators allege that regimes like the GDPR have negative effects on market structure, favoring already massive firms with substantial compliance departments, while overly burdening small businesses, thereby exacerbating trends toward corporate concentration (Gal & Aviv, 2020). Though they rarely break out the specific cost of IARs, critics suggest that the overall burden of compliance is so substantial that it weighs heavily against further expansion of data protection obligations.

Robust access rights will increase compliance costs. Clerical and legal personnel must administer access. Verifying the identity of requestors may

---

[44] See, for example, (DPcuria.eu, n.d.).

require special security measures (Ausloos et al., 2019; Iafrati, 2019).[45] For firms running on legacy information technology (IT) systems, reconfiguring software, and databases to generate reports on individual persons may require some investment (Fruchte, 2018; DataGrail, 2019). Describing automated decision-making systems accurately and accessibly may even require the development of new professional skills among compliance officers.

The mere listing of the various tasks and technology necessary to vindicate the rights of information access leads inexorably to consideration of its monetary costs. Experts in human resources can estimate the expected salary and benefits of the personnel needed to administer the right, licensing fees for software, insurance costs, and other ways of monetizing compliance costs. Such estimates have already informed and influenced debate over the GDPR.

Many critics of the GDPR have been focused on its costs. Pro-business think tanks have been particularly emphatic about what they allege are unsustainable compliance burdens (Layton, 2019), and in 2024 Mario Draghi blamed over-regulation in general for shortcomings in European competitiveness.[46] The Information Technology and Innovation Foundation (ITIF) has estimated that, among other costs, the "5,300,000 small businesses, 616,000 medium-sized businesses, and 19,000 large businesses" would need (respectively) 26,000, 15,000, and 10,000 data protection officers, and nonprofits would need another 8,000. Estimating a total cost of salary and fringe benefits of $107,000 per DPO per year for these 59,000 DPOs, the think tank projected a yearly cost of $6.37 billion for DPOs alone (Layton, 2019). It estimated that "federal legislation mirroring key provisions of the European Union's General Data Protection Regulation or California's Consumer Protection Act could cost the U.S. economy approximately $122 billion per year, or $483 per U.S. adult" (McQuinn & Castro, 2019). Of course, if the economic goal is maximization of Gross Domestic Product, such costs may be a boon to the economy rather than undermining it. Nevertheless, even in an economy already saturated with middlemen, there is a sense that the genuine productivity of the service economy is in question (Sapir, 2022; Fingleton, 1999). The precision of such

---

[45] Noting that different levels of verification may also be required. See in (Ausloos et al., 2019) discussing demanding verification standards, and argue that "the right to object or to restrict processing should, in general, require a lower burden of verification than access and erasure." See in (Iafrati, 2019) describing "the difficulty of operationalizing a verification process that properly balances confidentiality and control."

[46] See in (Layton, 2019) "the GDPR has proved cost prohibitive [for many firms and] the direct welfare loss is estimated be about €260 per European citizen. If a similar regulation were enacted in the US, total GDPR compliance costs for US firms alone could reach $150 billion, twice what the US spends on broadband network investment and one-third of annual e-commerce revenue in the US."

monetary figures is likely to be arresting to policymakers making decisions at the margin about whether to broaden or narrow the scope of access rights.

Of course, these projections are contestable. Especially for small and medium-sized businesses, aspects of compliance should become increasingly routinized and outsourced to expert contractors who operate at scale. If "regtech" and "govtech" have any promise, it is in automating routine compliance tasks. Compliance-enabling subroutines should also become more common in enterprise software as these firms vie for business. Human resources professionals should become more adept at compliance, adding to their skill set the types of knowledge about health and anti-discrimination law, and other rules that have become part of their domain. Nevertheless, it is important to acknowledge that no regulation is costless, and effecting truly comprehensive IARs may demand costly changes in business practices.

For example, one commentator has emphasized estimates that firms with over 500 employees will typically spend $3 million to comply with the GDPR (Shyy, 2021). Note that the GDPR is a complex set of laws, so only a small portion of these costs may have been incurred due to the access rights that have been our main concern. However, given the prevalence of such budgetary estimates, any effort to expand such IARs will almost certainly be faced with cost concerns.

Less, but still substantial, costs have been reported for CCPA compliance–and this was before the expansion of rights in the CPRA initiative. The CCPA required the California Office of the Attorney General (COAG) to clarify certain duties that regulations potentially promulgated pursuant to the law created and to assess the economic impact of such regulations. When the office developed certain proposed clarifications for notices to consumers, the handling of consumer requests, rules regarding minors, and nondiscrimination, these proposed regulations were subject to a "Standardized Regulatory Impact Assessment" (SRIA) (Office of the Attorney General, 2018). The SRIA was triggered because these steps were deemed to be "major regulation" whose impact "is expected to exceed $50 million per year once fully implemented" (Office of the Attorney General, 2018). The authors of the report stated that "Both the direct compliance costs and direct benefit of the proposed regulation are independently expected to exceed this threshold" (Office of the Attorney General, 2018). However, the report does not explain how the benefits were calculated to exceed $50 million per year.

Rather than focusing on benefits, the SRIA offered a lengthy and extensive extrapolation of the costs of privacy regulation. It offered only a brief and vague description of benefits. In an opening summary section, the SRIA offered a "preliminary estimate of direct compliance costs" of the proposed regulations at $467 million to $16.5 billion "over the next decade (2020–30), depending on the number of California businesses coming into compliance" (Office of the

Attorney General, 2018: 8). It provided no similar summary quantification of the economic value of the benefits of the clarifications and rules proposed by the COAG. The SRIA's authors did acknowledge that "the overall impact estimated here for CCPA excludes valuation of many offsetting non-pecuniary benefits and is therefore relatively pessimistic" (Office of the Attorney General, 2018: 45). They also remind readers that the magnitude of the compliance costs they address "is negligible from a macroeconomic perspective" (Office of the Attorney General, 2018: 45). Nevertheless, the pages of precise extrapolation of costs with numerical tables, compared with a brief and cursory list of benefits, sends a clear message to readers: costs are so direct and impactful that they merit quantification, whereas rigorous methods cannot similarly measure benefits (Pasquale, 2023).

Critics of expansive privacy regulations have called for more cost-benefit analysis to avoid excessively burdensome regulation (Thierer, 2013). Adam Thierer traces these calls back to FTC Commissioner Orson Swindle, who objected that there was "no consideration of the costs and benefits of regulation" in the FTC report "Privacy Online: Fair Information Practices in the Electronic Marketplace" (Federal Trade Commission, 2000). Swindle's dissent lambasted the FTC majority for publishing an "embarrassingly flawed" report, largely because he believed they had recommended legislation requiring websites to offer users notice, choice, and security protections, without adequately acknowledging the costs these requirements could impose. Former Commissioner Swindle looked particularly to the then-recent passage of the Children's Online Privacy Protection Act (COPPA) as a harbinger of high costs, should Congress follow the FTC's advice (Federal Trade Commission, 2000).[47]

Building on concerns like Swindle's, Thierer proposes a typology of costs to be taken into account by regulators as they interpret privacy statutes. These include costs to producers of digital services, costs to consumers, negative effects on market structure, and restrictions on freedom of expression. Thierer acknowledges that there are also benefits to privacy protections, such as enhancing consumer trust. However, he finds the discussion of the benefits of privacy in general to be "riddled with emotional appeals and highly subjective assertions of harm" (Thierer, 2013: 1066). Having documented what, to him, seem to be very solid and quantifiable direct monetary costs of privacy protections, and

---

[47] Noting in (Federal Trade Commission, 2000), in a dissenting statement, that "COPPA regulations require detailed Notice; Access, including the ability to review, correct, and delete information maintained by the site; and a form of opt-in mandated Choice (verifiable parental consent)" ("Dissenting Statement of Commissioner Swindle"). Swindle cited news stories to validate his concerns, including "New Children's Privacy Rules Pose Obstacles for Some Sites," *Wall St. J.*, April 24, 2000, at B-8 (which included a lawyer's estimate that her clients would need to spend between $60,000 and $100,000 annually to be compliant with COPPA).

vague and evanescent benefits, Thierer concludes that alternatives to regulation, like education and awareness building (including agency's publishing their own research on regulated firms' practices), self-help solutions (like code to block data collection), and self-regulation, are preferable in the digital privacy context.

As IARs advance, we should expect to see more arguments like Thierer's pressed on legislators and regulators. Indeed, emphasis on the costs of privacy has already become a key think argument for skeptics (Rinehart, 2022; Technet, 2023). This could lead to suboptimal data protection since cost-benefit analysis is prone to miss many critical benefits of data protection regulation (Nehf, 2005).[48] Given this imbalance, cost-benefit comparisons in areas as difficult to monetize as data protection should give way to (or at least be complemented by) more nuanced and narrative accounts of the types of futures that regulation and nonregulation will make more likely (Beckert, 2017).[49] Whether described as "scenario analyses" or "informal cost-benefit analysis," such qualitative assessments deserve a more important role in the policy evaluation landscape (Pasquale, 2023). Section 4 describes some key aspects of the content that should populate such qualitative analyses, to give a fairer picture of the overall impact of IARs (and other data regulations).

Quantifying costs and benefits is difficult, and may presume a "view from nowhere" merely affecting (rather than embodying) objectivity (Kysar, 2010). As economist Frank Ackerman and law professor Lisa Heinzerling have argued:

> The basic problem with narrow economic analysis of health and environmental protection is that human life, health, and nature cannot be described meaningfully in monetary terms; they are priceless. When the question is whether to allow one person to hurt another, or to destroy a natural resource; when a life or a landscape cannot be replaced; when harms stretch out over decades or even generations; when outcomes are uncertain; when risks are shared or resources are used in common; when the people 'buying' harms have no relationship with the people actually harmed–then we are in the realm of the priceless, where market values tell us little about the social values at stake. (Ackerman & Heinzerling, 2004: 9)

---

[48] Noting in (Nehf, 2005), "the costs of data proliferation will seldom be readily identifiable and ... the benefits of data protection will seldom be quantifiable."

[49] Practitioners of such methods should also bear in mind the propensity of prediction to generate self-fulfilling prophecies. Policy evaluations that posit strong responsiveness to IARs are likely to motivate regulators to ensure robust enough versions of the rights to make such responsiveness worthwhile. On the other hand, pessimistic forecasts are a prelude to disinvestment in enforcement of IARs by regulators.

The realm of environmental protection may seem far afield from that of privacy law, limiting the force of Ackerman's and Heinzerling's insight here. However, both fields of law arose out of the failures of other legal regimes to fully account for the harms generated by new forms of business.[50] As Dennis Hirsch explains, "just as the law had to adapt to changes during the Industrial Revolution" to either prevent or compensate for pollution caused by manufacturing, the law today is "struggling to address the privacy damage of the Information Age" (Hirsch, 2006). In a similar manner, the movement for "cultural environmentalism" in intellectual property policy broadened the view of legislators and regulators, shifting them away from thinking of copyright and patent laws as mere compromises among rival industrial factions, and more toward considering the impact of such laws on society as a whole (Pasquale, 2005; Boyle, 2007).

Like environmentalists, privacy activists have also been accused of failing to take into account the full economic impact of regulations. As Hirsch puts it:

> Privacy regulation today finds itself in a debate similar to the one that the environmental field has been engaged in for years. On the one hand, there is a growing sense that the digital age is causing unprecedented damage to privacy and that action must be taken immediately to mitigate these injuries. On the other, a chorus of voices warns against the dangers of imposing intrusive and costly regulation on the emerging business sectors of the information economy. (Hirsch, 2006: 9)

As privacy laws expand, the same types of cost-benefit analysis that have constrained environmental regulation are likely to become increasingly common in policymakers' mental models of data protection law's regulatory impact. Even worse, environmental laws in the US had at least a decade or so to prove their worth before CBA began to constrain them in earnest, while privacy protection may be nipped in the bud. Yet CBA as a mode of policy evaluation has important limits, particularly when it comes to the assessment of long-term, social benefits.

Many of the costs of regulating pollution are immediate, direct, and quantifiable: for example, the price of sourcing alternative fuel sources, or cleaner manufacturing processes. The benefits of reducing pollution are diffuse, long-term, and have taken many years to measure effectively (Shindell, 2020). The Environmental Protection Agency has often found it difficult or impossible to quantify a wide range of vital benefits (Masur & Posner, 2016). We have likely

---

[50] Like environmental regulation, data protection law covering corporate entities has long straddled the private/public law divide. Many data gathering relationships are governed by a contract – the "terms of service" that usually include a "privacy policy" (or, more accurately, "data collection policy") describing what data a firm will gather, and how it will use it. Numerous statutes also govern data, and either supersede or displace contracts, in many sectoral areas, ranging from finance to health care to telecommunications. The Federal Trade Commission also has authority to police unfair and deceptive practices, including terms of service.

under-regulated air pollution for decades as a result. As David Roberts observed in 2020, over the past several years, "the air pollution case has grown stronger and stronger, as the science on air pollution has advanced by leaps and bounds. Researchers are now much more able to pinpoint air pollution's direct and indirect effects, and the news has been uniformly bad" (Roberts, 2020). As the business models of privacy-invasive companies finally come under judicial scrutiny, it is quite possible that similar levels of harm will be found, even if they are more psychological and social than somatic.

This lagging documentation of harms and benefits leads to predictable imbalances and biases in policy evaluation. Amy Sinden has aptly described the tendency to quantify costs extensively, while only selectively or partially quantifying benefits, as a form of "false formality" (Sinden, 2015). A policy evaluator gains the trappings of mathematical rigor, while presenting a fundamentally inaccurate accounting. Only one side of the ledger is elaborately and precisely quantified in monetary values, while the other is left unmathematicized (Sinden, 2015: 143). This was the case with California SRIA for proposed privacy regulations discussed previously: it gave decision-makers a comprehensive sense of the economic costs, without doing the same for benefits.

There is ample legal authority for expanding the analysis here. A 2024 SRIA addressing, among other things, proposed regulations on consumers' rights to access data and to opt out of automated decisionmaking technology, offered a lengthier account of the expected benefits of the regulations. The California statute authorizing standardized regulatory impact analysis requires methodologies for "[a]ssessing and determining the benefits and costs of the proposed regulation, expressed in monetary terms to the extent feasible and appropriate," but also notes the importance of "[a]ssessing the value of nonmonetary benefits such as the protection of public health and safety, worker safety, or the environment, the prevention of discrimination, the promotion of fairness or social equity, the increase in the openness and transparency of business and government and other nonmonetary benefits consistent with the statutory policy or other provisions of law" (Cal. Gov. Code 2022, § 11346.36(b)(1)). Relatively complete and quantified lists of costs, when combined with partial and largely unquantified lists of benefits, results in what Sinden labels a false formality, which pretends to (but does not actually accomplish) scientific precision.

False formality fails on two levels. First, as Sinden observes, there is an immanent critique: the ostensibly rigorous method of comparing monetized costs and benefits is not actually being followed if there is no serious effort to monetize one side of the ledger. Second, there is deep irony in a fundamentally algorithmic method like formal cost-benefit analysis crimping regulatory efforts to promote algorithmic accountability via data protection law. Laws like the

CPRA and GDPR were passed in part because of widespread recognition that scoring, predictive analytics, and algorithms can be biased thanks to inadequate or unbalanced data. Mechanical calculation of costs that leaves benefits under or un-specified, is itself a biased algorithm (Chamayou, 2021; Berman, 2022). Policy evaluation tools like cost-benefit analysis should be subject to rules regarding algorithmic accountability, rather than being used as a cudgel to prematurely reduce their scope and impact.

Another irony of policy evaluation here is the role of IARs in generating the very data necessary to complete sound policy evaluation in the first place. At least in most substantive areas of regulation governed by cost-benefit analyses, one key rationale for the policy evaluation is the extra information that such evaluation brings to the regulatory process. Yet IARs are themselves a tool for exposing more data about commercial transactions and judgments. It is exceedingly difficult to complete a formal CBA of an information-forcing tool, since the tool itself is necessary to expose the range and intensity of the types of concerns that led to its codification into law.

Fortunately, there are less formal modes of policy evaluation with greater promise for recognizing the full range of benefits of IARs. The California SRIA critiqued earlier may be fruitfully compared with a landmark European assessment of the impact of data protection rules. Well before the GDPR went into effect, the European Commission released an impact assessment (IA) designed to assess the consequences of its plan for "a stronger and more coherent data protection [to] put individuals in control of their own data and reinforce legal and practical certainty for economic operators and public authorities" (European Commission, 2012: 40).[51] The EU IA emphasized the GDPR as a tool for unifying the internal market by harmonizing discordant or redundant member state rules (European Commission, 2012: 40). It also articulated an industrial policy to promote data-driven economic practices that respect the rights and interests of all participants in the economy (European Commission, 2012: 40).

The Commission's approach anticipates the type of scenario analysis that will help policymakers better understand the full range of potential benefits arising out of IARs. Scenario analysis entails extended narrative projection of how a given policy decision will increase the likelihood of some complex set of consequences, and decrease that of others (Ringland, 1998; Chermack et al., 2001; Andersson, 2018; Pasquale, 2023). In the rich and growing literature on algorithmic accountability, "algorithmic impact assessments" and audits are already beginning to include some of these narrative and qualitative elements

---

[51] The language cited was bold and italicized in the original document, to mark its foundational importance to the Commission's vision. It is reiterated in the Commission's statement of policy objectives.

(Selbst, 2021; Ada Lovelace Institute, 2022). Such rich and contextual analysis should replace the pro forma, brief, and individualistic mentions of data protection's benefits in documents like the 2018 SRIA from California discussed previously (Office of the Attorney General, 2018).

Evaluation of potential changes to information law necessitates multifaceted policy evaluation. Prematurely narrowing the inquiry by only considering monetizable costs and benefits cuts short what ought to be a richer and more complex process of policy evaluation (Stone, 2011). The key point now is to "broaden the view," both in terms of time and space, of what individual-level disclosures and submissions to government monitors can provide. Difficulties in monetary valuation do not necessarily indicate the lack of value of IARs; they can just as readily be interpreted as indications that such valuation is not an appropriate way to conduct policy evaluation for the interpretation of data protection laws. The next section charts a path toward such complex and nuanced policy evaluation, demonstrating varied ways of better taking into account the full range of benefits of IARs.

4 The Future of Information Access Rights: Empowering Civil Society and Social Reform

Critics' skepticism of data protection in general, and access rights in particular, gains force as interest focuses on the cost to firms to prepare for such access requests. A fair accounting of the effects of robust regimes of personal access rights demands attention to their benefits as well. To be sure, costs matter, and this section does not systematically dispute the alleged costs of IARs in particular, and privacy and data protection regulation in general. Rather, the focus here is on persistent lacunae in descriptions of benefits, since these gaps have characterized important policy evaluations and public interventions in data protection debates. There is little chance of wise interpretation of existing statutes, or effective drafting of future legislation, if those in positions of power do not fully understand the benefits of IARs. They not only assist individual consumers in understanding how they have been treated by corporations, and whether that treatment was fair or discriminatory, well-supported or groundless. They also promote socially beneficial forms of action.

IARs promise to alleviate long-standing psychological costs (including anxiety and frustration) at the "one-way mirrors" that frequently characterize corporate surveillance of persons (Ausloos & Dewitte, 2018). They have proven pivotal to several initiatives in collective education and action, as Section 4.2 documents. These effects may contribute to the development of aspects of industrial policy for the data economy, crafting markets in order to better reflect the contributions and risks of all participants. The use of IARs, publicity about concerning practices they expose, and activism for substantive reform to address these practices, will contribute to the independent political action necessary to support the ongoing development of democratic data policy. This can lead to a virtuous cycle of participation and reform, protecting key agencies from capture while educating citizens about their rights.[52]

4.1 How Individuals Benefit from Information Access Rights

Opaque digitization of judgment imposes predictable disutilities on those subject to its scrutiny. Not understanding the basis of an important decision can entail a dispiriting sense of powerlessness, not only undermining informational self-determination but also other important interests (Albers, 2014). Given the power of the private institutions that may be denying this information, the types of dignitary harms associated with denial of due process by the state are also possible here. As administrative law scholar Jerry L. Mashaw has observed (regarding dignitary theories in due process law), "the effects of process on participants, not just the rationality of substantive results, must be considered in judging the legitimacy of public decision-making " (Mashaw, 1981; see Hale, 1952 and Anderson, 2017, for applications to the private sector). In his foundational work shifting privacy discourse "from Orwell to Kafka," legal scholar Daniel J. Solove placed concerns about this type of alienating information asymmetry at the center of the data protection conversation (Solove, 2001).

Computerized rejections, accompanied with zero information about what went wrong for the applicant, are a prelude to a feeling of learned helplessness or "digital resignation" (Draper & Turow, 2019). From an instrumental perspective, there is no signal to suggest what to do to obtain a better outcome next time. There is also a troubling expressive dimension, a message that persons denied access to the relevant data or explanations are not worth the time of the firm judging them. This is an alienating experience, even if no one in the firm intended it to be so (Re & Solow-Niederman, 2019).[53]

Longstanding social norms and values have acclimated workers, borrowers, consumers, and many others to a sense of at least some degree of agency and

---

[52] In this way, the data protection movement may follow in the footsteps of the access to knowledge (A2K) movement (Kapczynski, 2008), which also relied on this type of "virtuous cycle" of information gathering, dissemination, and activism.

[53] As with Mashaw's reflections on due process above, there is much to learn from extant literature on the computerization of public judgments, when regulating private firms' algorithmic evaluations of persons. For example, just as alienation may follow if AI adjudicators perform "many discrete tasks presently assigned to human lawyers, judges, and juries, such as making legal arguments, ascertaining the credibility of witnesses, and setting the form and severity of punishment" (Re & Solow-Niederman, 2019), similar feelings of powerlessness may arise when private entities make critical decisions (about persons' fates as employees, students, borrowers, patients, and in other roles) in black boxed and unaccountable ways.

understanding in their interaction with managers, lenders, vendors, and other decision-makers. Indeed, this agency may be the most important sense of empowerment a person can feel in their daily experience of life (Anderson, 2017). When algorithmic mediation denies individuals the chance to look behind the curtain of social relations and understand what is going on, frustration follows.

This is a particular problem in the context of judgments based on secret data, which can feel like a modern-day star chamber. Consider, for instance, the story of a former Uber driver named Mansour, who gave a chilling description of his computer-mediated, gig economy workplace to a podcast in 2015 (Walker, 2015). When he had difficulties, Uber would never respond in person to him – it just sent form text messages and emails. This style of supervision was a series of take-it-or-leave-it ultimatums – a digital boss coded in advance (Calo & Rosenblat, 2017).[54] Then the company suddenly took a larger cut of revenues from him and other drivers, without a clear explanation. And finally, what seemed most outrageous to Mansour: his job could be terminated without notice if a few passengers gave him one-star reviews, since that could drag his average below 4.7. According to him, Uber had no real recourse for those stigmatized by a rating system that can instantly put a driver out of work – it simply crunched the numbers. This is a recipe for well-justified anxiety, however well it may enforce courteous service. Legal scholar Veena Dubal has expertly chronicled the intensification of this opaque regime over the past decade, calling algorithmic wage-setting a move from "gamification" to "gamblification" given how hard it is for workers to interpret the likely consequences of their actions (Dubal, 2024).

In their analysis of the harms arising from data breaches, Daniel J. Solove and Danielle Keats Citron elaborate on the experience of "risk and anxiety" arising out of out-of-control or "runaway" data (Solove & Citron, 2018). Dismayed by crabbed interpretations of standing doctrine (which tended to minimize or ignore the harms claimed by those whose privacy was violated), Solove and Citron powerfully articulate the harms caused by these intangible, but very real, harms. Cognizant of the risks posed by a data breach, many victims "spend time and money to mitigate the possibility of harm in the future" (Solove & Citron, 2018: 759). They know "a polluted credit report can interfere with [their] employment opportunities," and delay job searches accordingly.

Moreover, Solove and Citron convincingly argue that it "is rational for people to feel anxiety about the fact that their personal data is in the hands of criminals who can cause their financial ruin" (Solove & Citron, 2018: 766). Living in the

---

[54] This paragraph is drawn from (Pasquale, 2015a).

shadow of such grave threats is harmful in itself. Mateusz Grochowski has also skillfully extended the scope of aspiration in the field of digital vulnerability. He has made a well-documented case that consumer protection laws must move beyond a purely economic focus, to address issues that are now deemed noneconomic (including emotional and social well-being) (Grochowski, 2024). Grochowski observes that "EU consumer law has never developed a systematic framework for including non-economic interests and non-economic harm," despite an "expansion of the digital economy" that has "made this deficit particularly vivid and troublesome" (Grochowski, 2024: 196). This insight should be taken seriously by EU policymakers, particularly as the field of affective computing advances to develop more sophisticated methods of simulating and stimulating emotions (Pasquale, 2024).

Much the same can be said of frustrating opacity in important areas of decision-making in contemporary commercial life. Regulators can and should take into account the psychic costs that companies impose when their use of data for evaluative purposes is obscured from the persons they are evaluating. The growth of AI and ML threatens to exacerbate already troubling scenarios. In the old credit scoring regime, a savvy consumer could in principle keep up with factors added to evaluative algorithms, however unpredictable the exact impact of certain changes in variable values could be with respect to the final score. Confronted with a firm that gathers 12,000 data points for an algorithmic decision, the problem of making sense of a decision becomes commensurately more complex – and perhaps for many will seem insurmountable.

To be sure, some advocates of increasing algorithmatization would likely dismiss psychological costs (including risk, anxiety, and feelings of powerlessness before an evaluator or meaninglessness as to an evaluation) as exceedingly subjective, theoretical, or ideological concerns – or even a form of "robophobia" (Woods, 2022). However, these objections can be met, in ways that foreshadow the types of policy evaluation necessary to balance transparency requirements and business imperatives in the future.

Consider, first, the objection to subjective approaches to harm. Sometimes individual concerns are framed as lacking representativeness, mere "anecdata" or "trouble stories" without empirical backing (Ben-Shahar & Schneider, 2014). The implicit assumption behind such critiques is that any particular person's discomfort with a process is merely one person's opinion, until it is backed up by generalizable research and quantitative data based on observations of a representative sample of individuals, or, better, a randomized controlled trial. Demand for more rigorous forms of evidence is a hallmark of scientific inquiry. But it is also, in many present policy contexts, a way to tilt the playing field toward inaction, or to affirmatively advance the agenda of those entities with the resources to purchase, sponsor, or support the inquiry (Lacko, 2004; Kang, 2019; Revesz, 2020). By contrast, a phenomenological elaboration of the forms of objections that have arisen to black-boxed data practices is far more egalitarian. It may well be countered by stories of individuals who find black box computation more comforting and reassuring than potential alternatives, and that is to be expected. It is ultimately a simultaneously scientific, interpretive, and political judgment as to which of these accounts is more plausible and deserving of recognition in the regulatory process, not a mathematical problem of quantifying some utilitarian calculus of costs and benefits.

There are values beyond efficiency, including the opportunity to clarify one's values. Social theorist and privacy expert Julie E. Cohen describes privacy protections as "shelter[ing] dynamic, emergent subjectivity from the efforts of commercial and government actors to render individuals and communities fixed, transparent, and predictable" (Cohen, 2013; Richards, 2022).[55] Cohen's articulation here clarifies a core psychological cost of powerlessness: the fixity one can feel when it seems as though there is no way to question key institutions that are using secret data to make decisions about one's fate.

Business theorists of AI applications have praised them as "prediction machines," capable of extraordinary powers of forecasting (Agrawal et al., 2018). Sometimes these feats of prediction are welcome, as when an online retailer's marketing department immediately suggests a good substitute for an out-of-stock item. But there are also numerous areas where predictability may work against consumers; for example, if the same retailer hikes prices for shoppers it has calculated will not bother to look elsewhere (Bar-Gill, 2019; Valentino-Devries et al., 2012).[56] The same could be said of advisory software calculating methods of maximizing work demanded, minimizing raises, and all manner of other "zero-sum" moves (Safak & Farrar, 2021).[57] However well they assist managers in the mastery of the business environment, they are not experienced as positive innovations to those "mastered" by them.

To be sure, the receipt of even wanted information can cause disutilities as well. In their book *More Than You Wanted to Know: The Failure of Mandated Disclosure*, Omri Ben-Shahar and Carl Schneider offer a litany of reasons why

---

[55] On modulation as a danger of excessive knowledge of individuals by powerful entities.
[56] Bar-Gill also collecting examples of personalized pricing and price discrimination (Bar-Gill, 2019: 218).
[57] See per Worker Info Exchange: "our aim is to develop a data trust to help disparate and distributed workforces to come together to aggregate their personal data at work and with a common understanding, begin the process of building real collective bargaining power. We believe worker data trusts and greater algorithmic transparency can go a long way to correcting the balance so workers can have a fairer deal . . . We have processed more than 500 subject access requests over the last eight months on behalf of workers at Amazon Flex, Bolt, Deliveroo, Free Now, Just Eat, Ola and Uber" (Safak & Farrar, 2021).

elaborate descriptions of the terms of transactions may confuse, overburden, or frustrate consumers (Ben-Shahar & Schneider, 2014). Scholars working within their framework may characterize the data generated pursuant to IARs as just one more disclosure that does little to advance consumer interests, particularly given the high standard Ben-Shahar and Schneider set for evaluating any particular disclosure regime as efficient. However, there is a world of difference between the *mandated* disclosure criticized in *More Than You Wanted to Know*, and the exercise of IARs, which is done by particular persons in pursuit of particular information. This affirmative interest in information matters, reducing the burden on both businesses and those uninterested in how they have been characterized and judged by them. Indeed, in later work, Ben-Shahar (working with Ariel Porat) has been more open to personalization of disclosures as a path toward more targeted and efficient information sharing (Ben-Shahar & Porat, 2021).[58]

Of course, in monopolistic digital environments, it will be difficult, if not impossible, to negotiate for better terms based on what one has discovered. This is a problem competition law is presently addressing – and more access to data among those harmed by dominant platforms will likely create opportunities for better competition law enforcement and policy. Consumer protection authorities should also press for more alternative modes of evaluation to be made available to at least some subset of denied applicants or persons otherwise disadvantaged by algorithmic decision-making. Opportunities to make a narrative case for approval may be particularly meaningful, enhancing senses of agency and purpose (Pasquale & Kiriakos, 2025).

Research on contractual terms of service illuminates further dimensions of the information costs imposed by complex business practices, and how law may address the burdens they impose. For example, in their fascinating article "Pigouvian Contracts," Michael Simkovic and Meirav Furth argue that sellers are prone to develop complex contractual terms in order to take advantage of consumers (Simkovic & Furth, 2022). Simkovic and Furth justly complain that consumers are "encountering more contracts – and more complicated contracts – than it could possibly make sense for them to read and understand" (Simkovic & Furth, 2022: 7). To counteract that problem, they "encourage policymakers to make sellers internalize contract comprehension costs through quasi-Pigouvian taxation of sellers' contracts" (Simkovic & Furth, 2022: 8). Very complex data collection and processing by businesses also

---

[58] As they state, "warnings do not have to be so voluminous when each person cares, or ought to care, only about a small subset of the issues … People make bad choices for different reasons, and if the regulatory solution is to warn them, then it is better to communicate to each the relevant warning" (Ben-Shahar & Porat, 2021: 95–96).

impose burdens on both individuals (who may struggle to understand how they are being profiled) and society as a whole (when the corporate ends advanced by such practices exacerbates social problems). As Ben-Shahar has argued:

> Facebook's data practices [associated with the Cambridge Analytica scandal] lucidly illustrated the impact of data sharing on an ecosystem as a whole. When Facebook granted advertisers access to personal data, allowing them to distort voting decisions, the negative effect was not fully captured by private injuries to the specific individuals who received data-driven ads and whose voting was influenced (many of whom, indeed, regard themselves as unharmed). The critical negative effect was far broader, captured by the damage to an entire electoral and political environment, including nonprivacy-related harms and harms to other members of society. (Ben-Shahar, 2019: 106)

The very possibility of an application of Simkovic and Furth's work in the digital sphere puts the regulatory costs of implementing IARs in a new light: as a beneficial deterrent against exceedingly invasive or careless data gathering, and opaque data analysis and use. Even some firm insiders acknowledge how far "out of hand" data collection has gone. Consider this comment from a former Amazon chief information security officer (CISO), recalling his reaction to news about laws guaranteeing access rights: "I don't know how the hell we're going to deal with that, because we have no idea where our fucking data is" (Evans, 2021).[59] While billing themselves as trustworthy stewards of customer data, large internet firms are likely too sprawling and distributed to even keep track of their own uses of data. Access rights demand at least some minimal infrastructure of accountability.

When the CCPA was passed, skeptics believed few consumers would actually take advantage of the IARs it provided. We now know the skeptics were wrong. Thanks to reporting requirements embedded in the law for firms that hold data on at least 10 million Californians, commentators have documented 4.7 million access requests in the first year the CCPA was in effect. Large companies in the technology sector collectively accounted for 4.59 million of these, suggesting a leveling of the information playing field (Kimberley & Zetoony, 2021).[60] Of the remaining 110,000 or so requests, technology firms accounted for half, and firms in other sectors, the remainder.

---

[59] See in (Evans, 2021), a quote from the CISO.
[60] This is for the reporting period from July 1, 2020 to July 1, 2021. The focus of concern here on large firms suggests the US may see more proposals like the EU's DMA, which focuses on technology-intensive gatekeeper firms with over €7.5 billion in turnover in the European Economic Area.

Millions of access requests to large technology firms indicate widespread citizen interest in reclaiming some level of knowledge and control over their digital personae. It also takes some level of time and awareness-raising to convince more individuals to understand and use their rights (Ausloos, 2020). Moreover, even if few individuals actually use IARs, their impact can be large. In consumer transactions generally, there are many examples of small but informed minorities exercising positive influence on the market out of proportion to their size. As Yonathan Arbel and Roy Shapira have argued in their "Theory of the Nudnik," "consumers who call to complain ... post detailed online reviews, and file lawsuits" can "generate positive spillovers that reverberate throughout the economy" by calling attention to seller underperformance (Arbel & Shapira, 2020). "Nudnik" is a Yiddish term for a nagging or insistent person. Arbel and Shapira playfully invert its negative connotations to emphasize the social value of those willing to battle against harms or inconveniences that the vast majority of persons silently (if resentfully) bear. They predict that sellers may use big data to identify activist consumers in advance, and avoid doing business with them. Less intention-based discrimination is also possible, as algorithmic sorting mechanisms may simply "learn" to treat complaining customers worse than passive customers, if doing so leads to higher profits. This grim possibility presents yet another rationale for IARs: to give individuals the right to understand what data is held about them by companies even before they engage in a direct commercial relationship with the company.

Of course, once enough nudniks exercise their rights, journalists and the broader public tend to take notice. Max Schrems' decade-long legal battle against Facebook, initially enabled by his exercises of European IARs, exemplifies the importance of converting individual initiative to social activism in the data protection realm (Flor, 2021).[61] Many vocal consumers only find influence by coordinating with civil society groups and journalists. Their work will also be usefully advanced by robust IARs, giving rise to a second key category of benefits discussed in Section 4.2.

4.2 How Society Benefits from Information Access Rights

Online evaluations of consumers, workers, and other data subjects can be extraordinarily important, but also opaque. Recall the experience of the US Uber driver mentioned earlier, who found his confrontation with the "black box" of Uber data practices particularly frustrating. In Europe, by contrast, the NGO Worker Info Exchange has used IARs to help "balance the information-driven power

---

[61] See also Facebook's "Letter from Facebook User Operations–Data Access Request Team, to Max Schrems" (Facebook, 2011).

asymmetry between drivers and the company" (Open Society Foundations, 2019; Mahieu & Ausloos, 2020: 30). Workers wanted to know, for example, how often "surge pricing" luring them to a given area actually led to higher earnings, and how prioritization and bonus algorithms worked. In a court victory in 2021, the Dutch Supreme Court "rejected Uber's argument that drivers taking collective action to seek access to their data amounted to an abuse of data protection rights and confirmed the right of third parties including Worker Info Exchange, the ADCU and other trade unions to establish a gig workers data trust" (Worker Info Exchange, 2021).

The Worker Info Exchange case study is significant on two levels. First, it addresses concerns about individual data access rights exacerbating inequalities. Viewed from a purely individualistic and theoretical perspective, it may well be the case that relatively privileged and leisured persons have more time to examine and contest their records, or develop advocacy based on them. However, when civil society groups like Worker Info Exchange enter the picture, they help level the playing field, sharing the costs and leveraging the benefits of revelations. Similar action may also be a stepping stone toward more ambitious regulation of gig economy firms, which many commentators have called for (Dubal, 2017; Collier et al., 2017). As noted earlier, there were concerns about the scope of the victory here (Dubal, 2024). However, more expansive readings of the relevant law, and more active litigation and regulation, should open new doors of activism.

Second, the complex economic relationships characteristic of platform economics also increase the importance of access rights. In many jurisdictions, platform workers are recognized as employees. In others, platforms have succeeded in characterizing their workers not as employees, but as consumers of a service connecting those hiring and those seeking to be hired (Paul, 2017). Therefore, traditional protections guaranteed by employment law do not reach many of these so-called platform consumers. However, they do come under the protection of the CCPA. This enables another way of righting the balance disturbed by platforms' regulatory arbitrage around traditional worker protections (Niebler & Kern, 2020). Nor is this a one-off situation: both Fairtube and Turkopticon have demonstrated proof of wider interest (Niebler & Kern, 2020).

To their credit, European Commission staff anticipated such positive social effects in their impact assessment forecast of 2012. Commission staff stated that, in "cases concerning many persons, it should not be up to each data subject to pursue legal redress individually, but it should be possible to handle cases through associations, reducing effort for data controllers, individuals and the supervisory and judicial system" (European Commission, 2012). The extensive data subject access rights guaranteed pursuant to the GDPR are beginning to give a sense of the multiple, synergistic ways in which individual disclosures of data can catalyze larger research findings, civic education, and, in the long term, social change.

In exceptionally insightful research on the consequences of data access rights, René L. P. Mahieu and Jef Ausloos have identified collective action as essential to the effective enjoyment of data subject rights (Mahieu & Ausloos, 2020). In a submission to the European Commission, they compiled a long list of examples of this type of empowerment, ranging from investors organizing for redress after being mis-sold products from a bank, to consumers concerned about unfair personalized pricing, to citizens troubled by microtargeting of ads (Mahieu & Ausloos, 2020). Mahieu and Ausloos have also collected several compelling examples of activists using the pre-GDPR, 1995 Data Protection Directive (DPD) to gain access to important information. For example, they relate a case study of climate activists who suspected that British petroleum was spying on them. They ultimately did demonstrate that they were being monitored, and then BP had to turn over to them the personal records that the company had about them, pursuant to the DPD. Given the public attention such initiatives have attracted, they are much better characterized as examples of social and political action, than as simple acts of individuals attempting to better navigate the digital economy for personal advantage.

It is now incumbent on policymakers to take into account the rapidly changing information landscape, particularly given the rise of big data, AI, and ML. These technologies of information processing and provision may well make many extant complaints about the burden of disclosure outdated. So, too, do new ways of sharing information enable a new paradigm for transparency. This new paradigm characterizes disclosures as not only leveling the informational playing field in dyadic relationships (doctor/patient, borrower/lender, and intermediary/user), but rather, as informational infrastructure, which can create more forms of value for the community and the economy than siloed and privatized alternatives (Bietti, 2025). Associations in civil society, including news outlets and academic researchers, will be particularly important collaborators with citizens to ensure that access rights can be aggregated and coordinated in order to discern important patterns and propose plans for redress. While such benefits are contingent on social action, they nevertheless need to be part of a fair impact analysis of future clarifications and expansions of IARs via regulation.

Margot Kaminski has aptly characterized dual layers of citizen- and regulator-enforced data protection obligations "binary governance," and emphasized their complementarity (Kaminski, 2019a). So, too, are there synergistic and mutually reinforcing relationships between the exercise of personal access rights, good data governance, and vibrant civil society organizing. Stories of discrimination, unfair treatment, or insulting classifications have driven legislation guaranteeing access rights. It is critical for future interpretations and applications of extant data protection laws to address these issues.

IARs provide only tentative first steps toward addressing abuses of data, and must be complemented by many other interventions. However, they have already been used to shape technology and markets, catalyze collective action, and develop citizens' political awareness and agency. This is a track record worth extending, for the sake of both individual and collective self-determination.

5 Conclusion: Increasing the Dimensionality of Policy Evaluation with Respect to Data Protection

As novel databases and algorithms take on a more central role in allocating lower and higher loan interest rates, job offers and rejections, and benefits and burdens of all kinds, there will be growing demands for algorithmic transparency and fairness. Many public interest groups are advocating for increased transparency in this new digital economy of evaluative information (American Civil Liberties Institute, 2021).[62] Such transparency includes individuals' rights to access information held about them by corporations, as well as explanations of its processing and use.

Jurisdictions around the world are expanding IARs in response to the increasing number of digitized judgments affecting consumers, workers, borrowers, and internet users. As agencies and courts interpret and apply these rights, they face a growing backlash from critics who emphasize costs of compliance and minimize benefits. As policymakers weigh the costs and benefits of rights to information access, they need to bear in mind their social and long-term benefits, to fairly recognize their generative potential going forward. Associations in civil society, including news outlets and academic researchers, are particularly important collaborators with citizens to ensure that access rights can be aggregated and coordinated, to discern important patterns and propose plans for redress.

Regulators can better grapple with the difficult trade-offs posed by conflicts over the extent of access rights, by ensuring they have a full understanding of the benefits they bring. This Element has contributed to that balance by identifying social, psychological, and political benefits of IARs, beyond their use by

---

[62] The American Civil Liberties Union-led letter which the public interest groups joined includes extensive recommendations for policy reform. Over twenty-five non-governmental organizations signed on to it, representing many aspects of civil society.

particular individuals to better navigate finance, hiring, and other evaluative contexts. Gone are the days when a two-dimensional binary of business costs versus individual consumer benefits can adequately model the policy evaluation space here. Informed policy evaluation instead demands multidimensional, long-term, and values-informed approaches.

Despite their proven record and great potential, legal authorities granting access rights are now in danger of being interpreted very narrowly, or rarely enforced. This is a troubling development. Building habits of informed exercise of rights takes time and education. The costs of building this new intellectual infrastructure are immediate and obvious; the benefits are now hard to measure, only unfolding over an extended time frame. However, the precedents of worker and consumer self-organization described in Section 4 give regulators good reason to promote an infrastructure of data access by generously interpreting now-contested data access rights. When they were built, no one could guarantee that infrastructure like highways, railways, internet cables, and libraries would be widely used. Nevertheless, thanks to policymakers' willingness to recognize promising precedents and invest accordingly, we now all benefit from these infrastructures. The time for a similar investment in data access is now.

References

Ackerman, F. & Heinzerling, L. (2004). *Priceless: On Knowing the Price of Everything and the Value of Nothing*, New York: New Press.

ACM Conference (2024). *ACM Conference on Fairness, Accountability, and Transparency (ACM FAccT)*, https://facctconference.org/.

Ada Lovelace Institute (2022). *Algorithmic Impact Assessment: A Case Study in Healthcare*, London: Ada Lovelace Institute.

Adams-Prassl, J., Binns, R., & Kelly-Lyth, A. (2023). Directly Discriminatory Algorithms. *Modern Law Review*, 86(1), 144–175.

Agrawal, A., Gans, J., & Goldfarb, A. (2018). *Prediction Machines: The Simple Economics of Artificial Intelligence*, Boston: Harvard Business Review Press.

AI Now Institutute, NYU Law's Center on Race, Inequality, and the Law, and the Electronic Frontier Foundation (2018). *Litigating Algorithms: Challenging Government Use of Algorithmic Decision Systems*, New York: AI Now Institute.

Ajunwa, I. (2020a). The Black Box at Work. *Big Data & Society*, 7(2), 1–6.

Ajunwa, I. (2020b). The Paradox of Automation as Anti-Bias Intervention. *Cardozo Law Review*, 41(5), 1671–1742.

Ajunwa, I. (2021). An Auditing Imperative for Automated Hiring Systems. *Harvard Journal of Law & Technology*, 34(2), 621–700.

Albers, M. (2014). Realizing the Complexity of Data Protection. In Serge Gutwirth, S., Leenes, R., and De Hert, P., eds., *Reloading Data Protection: Multidisciplinary Insights and Contemporary Challenges*, New York: Springer, 213–235.

Allen, A. L. (2022). *Dismantling the 'Black Opticon': Privacy, Race Equity, and Online Data-Protection Reform*, New Haven: Yale Law Journal Forum.

American Civil Liberties Union, the Leadership Conference on Civil and Human Rights, Upturn, et al. (2021). Letter to the White House OSTP on Centering Civil Rights in AI Policy, www.aclu.org/sites/default/files/field_do cument/2021-07-13_letter_to_white_house_ostp_on_centering_civil_right s_in_ai_policy_1.pdf.

Ammermann, S. (2013). *Adverse Action Notice Requirements Under the ECOA and the FCRA*. https://consumercomplianceoutlook.org/2013/second-quar ter/adverse-action-notice-requirements-under-ecoa-fcra/.

Anderson, E. (2017). *Private Government: How Employers Rule Our Lives (and Why We Don't talk about It)*, Princeton: Princeton University Press.

Andersson, J. (2018). *The Future of the World Futurology, Futurists, and the Struggle for the Post-Cold War Imagination*, Oxford: Oxford University Press.

Angwin, J., Scheiber, N., & Tobin, A. (2017). *Facebook Job Ads Raise Concerns About Age Discrimination*, www.nytimes.com/2017/12/20/business/facebook-job-ads.html.

Aniceto, M. C., Barboza, F., & Kimura, H. (2020). Machine Learning Predictivity Applied to Consumer Creditworthiness. *Future Business Journal*, 6(1), 1–14.

Arbel, Y. A. & Shapira, R. (2020). Theory of the Nudnik: The Future of Consumer Activism and What We Can Do to Stop It. *Vanderbilt Law Review*, 73(4), 929–988.

Attorney-General's Department (2023). *Privacy Act Review Report*, Australian Government Attorney-General's Department.

Ausloos, J. (2018). *Paul-Olivier Dehaye and the Raiders of the Lost Data*, www.law.kuleuven.be/citip/blog/paul-olivier-dehaye-and-the-raiders-of-the-lost-data/.

Ausloos, J. (2020). *The Right to Erasure in EU Data Protection Law: from Individual Rights to Effective* Oxford: Oxford University Press.

Ausloos, J. & Dewitte, P. (2018). Shattering One-Way Mirrors: Data Subject Access Rights in Practice. *International Data Privacy Law*, 8(1), 4–28.

Ausloos, J., Mahieu, R., & Veale, M. (2019). Getting Data Subject Rights Right. *Journal of Intellectual Property, Information Technology and Electronic Commerce Law*, 10(3), 283–309.

Balkin, J. M. (2016). Information Fiduciaries and the First Amendment. *U.C. Davis Law Review*, 49(4), 1183–1234.

Bar-Gill, O. (2019). Algorithmic Price Discrimination When Demand Is a Function of Both Preferences and (Mis)perceptions. *University of Chicago Law Review*, 86(2), 217–254.

Beckert., J. (2017). *Imagined Futures: Fictional Expectations and Capitalist Dynamics*, Cambridge, MA: Harvard University Press.

Bender, E. M., Gebru, T., McMillan-Major, A., & Shmitchell, S. (2021). *On the Dangers of Stochastic Parrots: Can Language Models Be Too Big?* Association for Computing Machinery, 610–623. https://dl.acm.org/doi/10.1145/3442188.3445922

Benjamin, R. (2019). *Race after Technology: Abolitionist Tools for the New Jim Code*, Cambridge: Polity.

Ben-Shahar, O. (2019). Data Pollution. *Journal of Legal Analysis*, 11(1), 104–159.

References

Ben-Shahar, O. & Porat, A. (2021). *Personalized Law: Different Rules for Different People*, New York: Oxford University Press.

Ben-Shahar, O. & Schneider, C. E. (2014). *More Than You Wanted to Know: The Failure of Mandated Disclosure*, Princeton, NJ: Princeton University Press.

Berman., E. P. (2022). *Thinking like an Economist: How Efficiency Replaced Equality in U.S. Public Policy*, Princeton, NJ: Princeton University Press.

Biden, J. R. (2023). *Executive Order on the Safe, Secure, and Trustworthy Development and Use of Artificial Intelligence*, Washington, D.C.: The White House.

Bietti, E. (2025). Data is Infrastructure. *Theoretical Inquiries in Law*, 26, 55–87.

Birhane, A., Kahembwe, E. & Prabhu, V. U. (2021). *Multimodal Datasets: Misogyny, Pornography, and Malignant Stereotypes*, https://arxiv.org/abs/2110.01963.

Blass, J. (2019). Algorithmic Advertising Discrimination. *Northwestern University Law Review*, 114(2), 415–468.

Bolder, D. J. (2018). *Credit-Risk Modelling: Theoretical Foundations, Diagnostic Tools, Practical Examples, and Numerical Recipes in Python*, Cham: Springer.

Boniface, C., Bielova, N., Fouad, I., Lauradoux, C., & Santos, C. (2019). Security Analysis of Subject Access Request Procedures: How to Authenticate Data Subjects Safely When They Request for Their Data. In Naldi, M., Bourka, A. & Italiano, F. G. et al., eds., *Privacy Technologies and Policy: 7th Annual Privacy Forum, APF 2019 Rome, Italy, June 13–14, 2019 Proceedings*. Switzerland AG: Springer, 182–210.

Boyle, J. (2007). Cultural Environmentalism and beyond. *Law and Contemporary Problems*, 70(2), 5–22.

Broussard, M. (2018). *Artificial Unintelligence: How Computers Misunderstand the World*, Cambridge, MA: The MIT Press.

Bruckner, M. A. (2018). The Promise and Perils of Algorithmic Lenders' Use of Big Data. *Chicago-Kent Law Review*, 93(1), 3–60.

California Privacy Protection Agency (2021). *Invitation for Preliminary Comments On Proposed Rulemaking under the California Privacy Rights Act Of 2020*, https://cppa.ca.gov/regulations/pdf/invitation_for_comments.pdf.

Calo, R. (2012). Against Notice Skepticism in Privacy (and Elsewhere). *Notre Dame Law Review*, 87(3), 1027–1072.

Calo, R. & Rosenblat, A. (2017). The Taking Economy: Uber, Information, and Power. *Columbia Law Review*, 117(6), 1623–1690.

Center for Democracy and Technology (2021). *Preliminary Comments on Proposed Rulemaking under the California Privacy Rights Act Of 2020*, https://cppa.ca.gov/regulations/pdf/preliminary_rulemaking_comments_4.pdf.

Chamayou, G. (2021). *The Ungovernable Society: A Genealogy of Authoritarian Liberalism*. English Edition. Medford, MA: Polity Press.

Chermack, T. J., Lyhnam, S., & Ruona, W. E. A. (2001). A Review of Scenario Planning Literature. *Future Research Quarterly*, 17, 7–31.

Christl, W. (2017). *How Companies Use Personal Data Against People*, Berlin: Cracked Labs.

Christl, W. & Spiekermann, S. (2016). *Networks of Control: A Report on Corporate Surveillance, Digital Tracking, Big Data & Privacy*, Berlin: Facultas Cracked Labs.

Church, D., Pullen, M., & Winn, J. K. (1999). Recent Developments Regarding U.S. and EU Regulation of Electronic Commerce. *International Lawyer (ABA)*, 33(2), 347–366.

Citron, D. K. (2010). Civil Rights in Our Information Age*: in The Offensive Internet: Speech, Privacy and Reputation*. Cambridge, MA: Harvard University Press.

Clifford, S. & Silver-Greenberg, J. (2013). *Retailers Track Employee Thefts in Vast Databases*, www.nytimes.com/2013/04/03/business/retailers-use-data bases-to-track-worker-thefts.html#:~:text=Facing%20a%20wave%20of% 20employee,working%20again%20in%20the%20industry.

Cohen, J. E. (2013). What Privacy is for. *Harvard Law Review*, 126(7), 1904–1933.

Collier, R. B., Carter, C., & Dubal, V. (2017). *Labor Platforms and Gig Work: The Failure to Regulate*, eScholarship, Berkeley, CA: University of California.

Consumer Financial Protection Bureau (n.d.). *Appendix C to Part 1002 – Sample Notification Forms*, www.consumerfinance.gov/rules-policy/regula tions/1002/c/.

Consumer Reports (2021). *Preliminary Comments on Proposed Rulemaking Under the California Privacy Rights Act Of 2020*, https://cppa.ca.gov/regula tions/pdf/preliminary_rulemaking_comments_4.pdf.

Costanza-Chock, S. (2020). *Design Justice: Community-Led Practices to Build the Worlds We Need*, Cambridge, MA: The MIT Press.

Dastin, J. (2018). *Amazon Scraps Secret AI Recruiting Tool That Showed Bias Against Wome*, www.reuters.com/article/idUSKCN1MK0AG/.

DataGrail (2019). *The Age of Privacy: The Cost of Continuous Compliance: Benchmarking the Ongoing Operational Impact of GDPR & CCPA*, www .datagrail.io/resources/reports/gdpr-ccpa-cost-report/.

Division of Financial Practices (2021). *Letter to Office of Fair Lending & Equal Opportunity Bureau of Consumer Financial Protection*, www.ftc.gov/system/files/documents/reports/ftc-enforcement-activities-under-ecoa-regulation-b-report-cfpb/p154802cfpbecoareport.pdf.

Dixon, P. & Gellman, R. (2014). *The Scoring of America: How Secret Consumer Scores Threaten Your Privacy and Your Future*, San Diego, CA: World Privacy Forum.

Doerr, M., Suver, C., & Wilbanks, J. (2016). *Developing a Transparent, Participant-Navigated Electronic Informed Consent for Mobile-Mediated Research*, https://papers.ssrn.com/sol3/papers.cfm?abstract_id=2769129.

DPcuria.eu (n.d.). *Referral C-203/22 (Dun & Bradstreet Austria, 16 Mar 2022)*, www.dpcuria.eu/case?reference=C-203/22.

Draper, N. & Turow, J. (2019). The Corporate Cultivation of Digital Resignation. *New Media and Societ*, 21(8), 1824–1839.

Dubal, V. (2024). On Algorithmic Wage Discrimination. *Columbia Law Review*, 123(7), 1929–1992.

Dubal, V. B. (2017). Wage Slave or Entrepreneur: Contesting the Dualism of Legal Worker Identities. *California Law Review*, 105(1), 65–124.

Dyal-Chand, R. (2021). Autocorrecting for Whiteness. *Boston University Law Review*, 101(1), 191–286.

Ebeling, M. F. E. (2016). *Healthcare and Big Data: Digital Specters and Phantom Objects*, New York: Palgrave Macmillan.

Ebeling, M. F. E. (2018). Uncanny Commodities: Policy and Compliance Implications for the Trade in Debt and Health Data. *Annals of Health Law*, 27(2), 125–148.

Edwards, L. & Veale, M. (2017). Slave to the Algorithm? Why a "Right to an Explanation" Is Probably Not the Remedy You Are Looking for. *Duke Law & Technology Review*, 16(1), 18–84.

EFF and ACLU (2021). *Preliminary Comments on Proposed Rulemaking Under the California Privacy Rights Act Of 2020*, https://cppa.ca.gov/regulations/pdf/preliminary_rulemaking_comments_1.pdf.

Epstein, A. (2015). *Facebook's New Patent Lets Lenders Reject a Loan Based on Your Friends' Credit Scores – But Don't Freak out*, https://qz.com/472751/facebooks-new-patent-lets-lenders-reject-a-loan-based-on-your-friends-credit-scores-but-dont-freak-out.

Eubanks, V. (2018). *Automating Inequality: How High-Tech Tools Profile, Police, and Punish the Poor*, New York: St. Martin's Press.

European Commission (2012). *Commission Staff Working Paper Impact Assessment Accompanying the document*, www.europarl.europa.eu/cmsdata/59702/att_20130508ATT65856-1873079025799224642.pdf.

European Commission (2017). *Article 29 Data Protection Working Party, Guidelines on Automated Individual Decision-Making And Profiling for the Purposes of Regulation 2016/679*, https://ec.europa.eu/newsroom/document.cfm?doc_id=47742.

European Data Protection Board (2022). *Guidelines 01/2022 on Data Subject rights – Right of Access*, https://edpb.europa.eu/our-work-tools/documents/public-consultations/2022/guidelines-012022-data-subject-rights-right_en.

Evans, W. (2021). *Inside Amazon's Failures to Protect Your Data: Internal Voyeurs, Bribery Scandals and Backdoor Schemes*, https://revealnews.org/article/inside-amazons-failures-to-protect-your-data-internal-voyeurs-bribery-schemes-and-backdoor-access/.

Eveleth, R. (2019). *Credit Scores Could Soon Get Eve Creepier and More Biased*, www.vice.com/en/article/zmpgp9/credit-scores-could-soon-get-even-creepier-and-more-biased.

Eykholt, K., Evtimov, I., Fernandes, E. et al. (2018). Robust Physical-World Attacks on Deep Learning Visual Classification. *2018 IEEE/CVF Conference on Computer Vision and Pattern Recognition CVPR Computer Vision and Pattern Recognition (CVPR), 2018 IEEE/CVF Conference*, 1625–1634.

Facebook (2011). *Letter from Facebook User Operations–Data Access Request Team, to Max Schrem*, www.europe-v-facebook.org/FB_E-Mails_28_9_11.pdf.

Federal Trade Commission (2000). *Privacy Online: Fair Information Practices in the Electronic Marketplace: A Federal Trade Commission Report to Congress*, Washington, D.C.: Federal Trade Commission.

Federal Trade Commission (2013). *In FTC Study, Five Percent of Consumers Had Errors on Their Credit Reports That Could Result in Less Favorable Terms for Loans*, www.ftc.gov/news-events/news/press-releases/2013/02/ftc-study-five-percent-consumers-had-errors-their-credit-reports-could-result-less-favorable-terms.

Fingleton, E. (1999). *In Praise of Hard Industries: Why Manufacturing, Not the Information Economy, Is the Key to Future Prosperity*, Boston, MA: Houghton Mifflin.

Fleischer, R. S. (2020). Bias In, Bias Out: Why Legislation Placing Requirements on the Procurement of Commercialized Facial Recognition Technology Must Be Passed to Protect People of Color. *Public Contract Law Journal*, 50(1), 63–89.

Flor, A. (2021). The Impact of Schrems II: Next Steps for U.S. Data Privacy Law. *Notre Dame Law Review*, 96(5), 2035–2058.

Foohey, P. & Sternberg Greene, S. (2021). Credit Scoring Duality. *Law & Contemporary Problems*, 85, 101–121.

Fourcade, F. & Healy, K. (2024). *The Ordinal Society.* Cambridge, MA: Harvard University Press.

Fowler, G. A. (2020). *Don't Sell My Data! We Finally Have a Law for That*, www.washingtonpost.com/technology/2020/02/06/ccpa-faq/.

Franks, M. A. (2019). *The Cult of the Constitution.* Stanford, CA: Stanford University Press.

Fruchte, J. (2018). *Cost of GDPR Compliance for a Small Software Business*, https://medium.com/expected-behavior/cost-of-gdpr-compliance-for-a-small-software-business-eb2b8b8e829.

Gal, M. & Aviv, O. (2020). The Competitive Effects of the GDPR. *Journal of Competition Law and Economics*, 16(3), 349–391.

Gellert, R., Bekkum, M. V., & Borgesius, F. Z. (2021). *The Ola & Uber Judgments: for the First Time a Court Recognises a GDPR Right to an Explanation for Algorithmic Decision-Making*, http://eulawanalysis.blogspot.com/2021/04/the-ola-uber-judgments-for-first-time.html.

Gershgorn, D. (2018). *If AI Is Going to be the World's Doctor, It Needs Better Textbooks*, https://qz.com/1367177/if-ai-is-going-to-be-the-worlds-doctor-it-needs-better-textbooks.

Gibbs, S. (2015). *Women Less Likely to be Shown Ads for High-Paid Jobs on Google, Study Shows*, www.theguardian.com/technology/2015/jul/08/women-less-likely-ads-high-paid-jobs-google-study.

Gilbert, T. K., Dean, S., Zick, T., & Lambert, N. (2022). *Choices, Risks, and Reward Reports: Charting Public Policy for Reinforcement Learning Systems*, CLTC Centre for Long-Term Cybersecutiry, University of California, Berkeley.

Google (2021). *Preliminary Comments on Proposed Rulemaking Under the California Privacy Rights Act of 2020*, https://cppa.ca.gov/regulations/pdf/preliminary_rulemaking_comments_1.pdf.

Grimmelmann, J. & Westreich, D. (2017). Incomprehensible Discrimination. *California Law Review Online*, 7, 164–177.

Grochowski, M. (2024). Digital Vulnerability in a Post-Consumer Society. Subverting Paradigms? In Camilla Crea and Alberto De Franceschi, eds., *Digital Vulnerability in European Private Law.* Nomos, Germany, 221–225.

Gunter, K. G. (2000). Computerized Credit Scoring's Effect on the Lending Industry. *North Carolina Banking Institute*, 4, 443–474.

Guzelian, C. P. (2008). Scientific Speech. *Iowa Law Review*, 93(3), 881–928.

Hale., R. L. (1952). *Freedom through Law: Public Control of Private Governing Power*, New York: Columbia University Press.

Hardy, Q. (2012). *Just the Facts. Yes, All of Them*, https://archive.nytimes.com/query.nytimes.com/gst/fullpage-9A0CE7DD153CF936A15750C0A9649D8B63.html.

Hartzog, W. & Richards, N. (2020). Privacy's Constitutional Moment and the Limits of Data Protection. *Boston College Law Review*, 61(5), 1687–1762.

Havard, C. J. (2011). On the Take: The Black Box of Credit Scoring and Mortgage Discrimination. *Boston University Public Interest Law Journal*, 20(2), 241–288.

Hernandez, G. A., Eddy, K. J., & Muchmore, J. (2001). Insurance Weblining and Unfair Discrimination in Cyberspace. *SMU Law Review*, 54(4), 1953–1972.

Hildebrandt, M. (2012). The Dawn of a Critical Transparency Right for the Profiling Era. *Digital Enlightenment Yearbook 2012*, Amsterdam: IOS Press.

Hiller, J. S. & Jones, L. S. (2022). Who's Keeping Score? Oversight of Changing Consumer Credit Infrastructure. *American Business Law Journal*, 59(1), 61–122.

Hirsch, D. D. (2006). Protecting the Inner Environment: What Privacy Regulation Can Learn from Environmental Law. *Georgia Law Review*, 41(1), 1–64.

Hoffman, S. (2018). Big Data's New Discrimination Threats: Amending the Americans with Disabilities Act to Cover Discrimination Based on Data-Driven Predictions of Future Diseas. In Cohen, I. Glenn, Lynch, H. F., Vayena, E., and Gasser, U., eds., *Big Data, Health Law, and Bioethics*, Cambridge: Cambridge University Press, 85–97.

Hoffman, S. & Podgurski, A. (2020). Artificial Intelligence and Discrimination in Health Care. *Yale Journal of Health Policy, Law and Ethics*, 19(3), 1–49.

Hurley, M. & Adebayo, J. (2016). Credit Scoring in the Era of Big Data. *Yale Journal of Law & Technology*, 18(2), 148–216.

Iafrati, R. (2019). Can the CCPA Access Right Be Saved? Realigning Incentives in Access Request Verification. *Pittsburgh Journal of Technology Law and Policy*, 20, 25–42.

Jee, C. (2019). *A Biased Medical Algorithm Favored White People for Health-Care Programs*, www.technologyreview.com/2019/10/25/132184/a-biased-medical-algorithm-favored-white-people-for-healthcare-programs/.

Kahneman, D., Sibony, O., & Sunstein, C. R. (2021). *Noise: A Flaw in Human Judgment*, New York: William Collins; Little, Brown Spark.

Kaminski, M. E. (2019a). Binary Governance: Lessons from the GDPR's Approach to Algorithmic Accountability. *Southern California Law Review*, 92(6), 1529–1616.

Kaminski, M. E. (2019b). The Right to Explanation, Explained. *Berkeley Technology Law Journal*, 34(1), 189–218.

Kaminski, M. E. & Malgieri, G. (2020). *Multi-layered Explanations from Algorithmic Impact Assessments in the GDPR at "FAT* '20: Proceedings of the 2020 Conference on Fairness, Accountability, and Transparency*," Association for Computing Machinery, 68–79.

Kang, Y. (2019). Secret Science and the Environmental Protection Agency's Postmodern Attack on Agency Decision-Making. *Journal of Land Use & Environmental Law*, 35(1), 69–90.

Kapczynski, A. (2008). The Access to Knowledge Mobilization and the New Politics of Intellectual Property. *Yale Law Journal*, 117(5), 804–885.

Katyal, S. K. (2019). Private Accountability in the Age of Artificial Intelligence. *UCLA Law Review*, 66(1), 54–141.

Kimberley, B. & Zetoony, D. (2021). *The Brave New World of Data Privacy: Benchmarking Corporate Compliance*, https://docket.acc.com/brave-new-world-data-privacy-benchmarking-corporate-compliance.

Kysar., D. A. (2010). *Regulating from Nowhere: Environmental Law and the Search for Objectivity*, New Haven, CT: Yale University Press.

Lacko, M. V. (2004). The Data Quality Act: Prologue to a Farce or a Tragedy. *Emory Law Journal*, 53(1), 305–358.

Lauer, J. (2017). *Creditworthy: A History of Consumer Surveillance and Financial Identity in America*, New York: Columbia University Press.

Layton, R. (2019). *The 10 Problems of the GDPR: The US can Learn from the EU's Mistakes and Leapfrog Its Policy*, www.judiciary.senate.gov/imo/media/doc/Layton%20Testimony.pdf.

Lee, K.-F. & Chen, Q.-F. (2021). *AI 2041*, New York: Currency.

Lehr, D. & Ohm, P. (2017). Playing with the Data: What Legal Scholars Should Learn about Machine Learning. *U.C. Davis Law Review*, 51(2), 653–718.

Federal Trade Commission. (2012). *Report to Congress under Section 319 of the Fair and Accurate Credit Transactions Act of 2003*, Washington, D.C.

Linardatos, P., Kotsiantis, S., & Papastefanopoulos, V. (2021). Explainable AI: A Review of Machine Learning Interpretability Methods. *Entropy*, 23(1), 1–45.

Lou, Y., Caruana, R., Gehrke, J., & Hooker, G. (2013). *Accurate Intelligible Models with Pairwise Interactions at "KDD '13: Proceedings of the 19th ACM SIGKDD InternationalCconference on Knowledge Discovery and Data Mining*," Association for Computing Machinery, 623–631.

Mahieu, R. L. P. & Ausloos, J. (2020). *Harnessing the Collective Potential of GDPR Access Rights: Towards an Ecology of Transparency*, https://pure.uva.nl/ws/files/58628461/Harnessing_the_collective_potential_of_GDPR_access_rights_towards_an_ecology_of.pdf.

Mahieu, R. L. P. & Ausloos, J. (2020). *Recognising and Enabling the Collective Dimension of the GDPR and the Right of Access*, https://osf.io/preprints/lawarxiv/b5dwm.

Malgieri, G. & Comandé, G. (2017). Why a Right to Legibility of Automated Decision-Making Exists in the General Data Protection Regulatio. *International Data Privacy Law*, 7(4), 243–265.

Mandinaud, V. & Ponce Del Castillo, A. (2024). AI Systems, Risks and Working Conditions. In Ponce del Castillo, A., ed., *Artificial Intelligence, Labour and Society*. Brussels: ETUI Press, 237–249.

Marcus, G. & Davis, E. (2019). *Rebooting AI: Building Artificial Intelligence We can Trust*, New York: Pantheon Books.

Marks, M. (2021). Emergent Medical Data: Health Information Inferred by Artificial Intelligence. *UC Irvine Law Review*, 11(4), 995–1066.

Mashaw, J. L. (1981). Administrative Due Process: The Quest for a Dignitary Theory. *Boston University Law Review*, 61(4), 885–931.

Masur, J. S. & Posner, E. A. (2016). Unquantified Benefits and the Problem of Regulation under Uncertainty. *Cornell Law Review*, 102(1), 87–138.

Mathews, K. J. & Bowman, C. M. (2018). *The California Consumer Privacy Act of 2018*, https://privacylaw.proskauer.com/2018/07/articles/data-privacy-laws/the-california-consumer-privacy-act-of-2018.

McQuinn, A. & Castro, D. (2019). *The Costs of an Unnecessarily Stringent Federal Data Privacy Law*, https://itif.org/publications/2019/08/05/costs-unnecessarily-stringent-federal-data-privacy-law/.

Mittelstadt, B., Russell, C., & Wachter, S. (2019). *Explaining Explanations in AI at "FAT* '19: Proceedings of the Conference on Fairness, Accountability, and Transparency,"* Association for Computing Machinery, 279–288.

Monticollo, A., Cividanes, E., & Reckell, C. (2020). California Privacy Landscape Changes Again with Approval of New Ballot Initiative. *Antitrust Magazine*, 35(1), 32.

Moralidad, G. (2021). *Facebook Fired 52 Employees for Accessing User Data, Including Women They Like*, www.latintimes.com/facebook-fired-52-employees-accessing-user-data-including-women-they-477809.

Naudts, L., Ausloos, J., & Dewitte, P. (2022). Meaningful Transparency through Data Rights: A Multidimensional Analysis. In Kosta, E., Leenes, R., and Kamara, I. *Research Handbook on EU Data Protection Law*, Northampton, MA: Edward Elgar, 530–571.

Nehf, J. P. (2005). The Limits of Cost-Benefit Analysis in the Development of Database Privacy Policy in the United States. In I. Ramsay, ed., *Risk and Choice in Consumer Society*, Bruxelles: Ant. N. Sakkoulas; Bruylant, 61–88.

Niebler, V. & Kern, A. (2020). *Organizing YouTube: A Novel Case of Platform Worker Organizing*, Berlin: Friedrich Ebert Stiftung.

Nissenbaum, H. (1996). Accountability in a Computerized Society. *Science and Engineering Ethics*, 2(1), 25–42.

Nissenbaum, H. (2004). Privacy as Contextual Integrity. *Washington Law Review*, 79(1), 119–158.

Obermeyer, Z., Mullainathan, S., Vogeli, C., & Powers, B. (2019). Dissecting Racial Bias in an Algorithm Used to Manage the Health of Populations. *Science*, 366(6464), 447–453.

Office of Oversight and Investigations Majority Staff (2013). *A Review of the Data Broker Industry: Collection, Use, and Sale of Consumer Data for Marketing Purposes*, Washington, D.C.: United States Senate Committee on Commerce, Science, and Transportation.

Office of the Attorney General (2018). *Standardized Regulatory Impact Assessment*, U.S. Department of JUSTICE.

Olmstead, M. (2021). *A Prominent Priest Was Outed for Using Grindr. Experts Say It's a Warning Sign*, https://slate.com/technology/2021/07/catholic-priest-grindr-data-privacy.html.

O'Neil, C. (2016). *Weapons of Math Destruction: How Big Data Increases Inequality and Threatens Democracy*, New York: Crown.

Open Society Foundations (2019). *Q&A: Fighting for Workers' Right to Data*, www.opensocietyfoundations.org/voices/q-and-a-fighting-for-workers-right-to-data.

Organisation for Economic Co-operation and Development (1980). *OECD Guidelines on the Protection of Privacy and Transborder Flows of Personal Data*.

Paleja, A. (2021). *Google Fires 80 Employees for Exploiting User Data*, https://interestingengineering.com/google-fires-80-employees-for-exploiting-user-data.

Pardau, S. L. (2018). The California Consumer Privacy Act: Towards a European-Style Privacy Regime in the United States. *Journal of Technology Law & Policy*, 23(1), 68–114.

Pasquale, F. (2005). Toward an Ecology of Intellectual Property: Lessons from Environmental Economics for Valuing Copyright's Commons. *Yale Journal of Law & Technology*, 8, 78–135.

Pasquale, F. (2015). *The Black Box Society: The Secret Algorithms that Control Money and Information*, Cambridge, MA: Harvard University Press.

Pasquale, F. (2018). Law and Technology When Machine Learning is Facially Invalid. *Communications of the ACM*, 61(9), 25–27.

Pasquale, F. (2020). *New Laws of Robotics: Defending Human Expertise in the Age of AI*. Cambridge, MA: The Belknap Press of Harvard University Press.

Pasquale, F. (2023). Power and Knowledge in Policy Evaluation: From Managing Budgets to Analyzing Scenarios. *Law & Contemporary Problems*, 86 (3), 39–69.

Pasquale, F. (2024). Affective Computing at Work: Rationales for Regulating Emotion Attribution and Manipulation. In Ponce del Castillo, A., ed., *Artificial Intelligence, Labour and Society*. Brussels: ETUI Press, 175–179.

Pasquale, F. & Citron, D. K. (2014). Promoting Innovation While Preventing Discrimination: Policy Goals for the Scored Society. *Washington Law Review*, 89(4), 1413–1424.

Pasquale, F. (2015a). Digital Star Chamber. *Aeon*, https://aeon.co/essays/judge-jury-and-executioner-the-unaccountable-algorithm.

Pasquale, F. & Kiriakos, M. (2025). Contesting the Inevitability of Scoring: The Value(s) of Narrative in Consumer Credit Allocation. In Burchard C. & Spiecker I., eds., *Algorithmic Transformations of Power: Between Trust, Conflict, and Uncertainty*. Nomos/Hart, MI: forthcoming.

Paul, K. (2020). *They Know Us Better Than We Know Ourselves': How Amazon Tracked My Last Two Years of Reading*, www.theguardian.com/technology/2020/feb/03/amazon-kindle-data-reading-tracking-privacy.

Paul, S. M. (2017). Uber as For-Profit Hiring Hall: A Price-Fixing Paradox and its Implications. *Berkeley Journal of Employment and Labor Law*, 38(2), 233–263.

Pearl, J. & Mackenzie, D. (2019). *The Book of Why: The New Science of Cause and Effect*. London: Penguin Books.

Pettypiece, S. & Robertson, J. (2014a). *How Big Data's 'Suffering Seniors' List Peers into Medicine Chests*, https://scnow.com/business/how-big-datas-suffering-seniors-list-peers-into-medicine-chests/article_87a6d21e-39df-11e4-81ea-001a4bcf6878.html.

Pettypiece, S. & Robertson, J. (2014b). *Sick Elderly for Sale by Data Miners for 15 Cents a Name*, www.bloomberg.com/news/articles/2014-09-11/how-big-data-peers-inside-your-medicine-chest.

Poon, M. (2009). From New Deal Institutions to Capital Markets: Commercial Consumer Risk Scores and the Making of Subprime Mortgage Finance. *Accounting, Organizations and Society*, 34(5), 654–674.

Privacy International (2017). *Case Study: Fintech and the Financial Exploitation of Customer Data*, www.privacyinternational.org/case-studies/757/case-study-fintech-and-financial-exploitation-customer-data.

Re, R. M. & Solow-Niederman, A. (2019). Developing Artificially Intelligent Justice. *Stanford Technology Law Review*, 22(2), 242–289.

Regalbuto, J. (2019). *Use of External Consumer Data and Information Sources in Underwriting for Life Insurance*, New York: New York State Department of Financial Services.

Revesz, R. L. (2020). Destabilizing Environmental Regulation: The Trump Administration's Concerted Attack on Regulatory Analysis. *Ecology Law Quarterly*, 47(3), 887–956.

Richards, N. (2022). *Why Privacy Matters*, New York: Oxford University Press.

Richards, N. & Hartzog, W. (2017). Trusting Big Data Research. *DePaul Law Review*, 66(2), 579–590.

Richardson, R., Crawford, K., & Schult, J. (2019). Dirty Data, Bad Predictions: How Civil Rights Violations Impact Police Data, Predictive Policing Systems, and Justice. *New York University Law Review*, 94, 192–233.

Rieke, A., Bogen, M., & Robinson, D. G. (2018). *Public Scrutiny of Automated Decisions: Early Lessons and Emerging Methods*, Washington, D.C.: Omidyar Network and Upturn.

Rinehart, W. (2022). *What is the Cost of Privacy Legislation?* www.thecgo.org/benchmark/what-is-the-cost-of-privacy-legislation/.

Ringland, G. (1998). *Scenario Planning Managing for the Future*, 1st Illustrated Reprint ed., New York: John Wiley.

Roberts, D. (2020). *Air Pollution is Much Worse than We Thought*, www.vox.com/energy-and-environment/2020/8/12/21361498/climate-change-air-pollution-us-india-china-deaths.

Rocket Mortgage (2021). *Preliminary Comments on Proposed Rulemaking under the California Privacy Rights Act Of 2020*, https://cppa.ca.gov/regulations/pdf/preliminary_rulemaking_comments_1.pdf.

Rostow, T. (2017). What Happens When an Acquaintance Buys Your Data: A New Privacy Harm in the Age of Data Broker. *Yale Journal on Regulation*, 34(2), 667–708.

Safak, C. & Farrar, J. (2021). *Managed by Bots: Data-Driven Exploitation in the Gig Economy*, London: Business & Human Rights Resource Centre.

Sapir, J. (2022). Assessing the Russian and Chinese Economies Geostrategically. *American Affairs Journal*, VI (4), https://americanaffairsjournal.org/2022/11/assessing-the-russian-and-chinese-economies-geostrategically/.

Schneider, V. (2020). Locked out by Big Data: How Big Data Algorithms and Machine Learning May Undermine Housing Justice. *Columbia Human Rights Law Review*, 52(1), 251–305.

Schüll, N. D. (2012). *Addiction by Design: Machine Gambling in Las Vegas*, Princeton, NJ: Princeton University Press.

Selbst, A. D. (2021). An Institutional View of Algorithmic Impact Assessments. *Harvard Journal of Law & Technology*, 35(1), 117–191.

Selbst, A. & Powles, J. (2017). Meaningful Information and the Right to Explanation. *International Data Privacy Law*, 7(4), 233–242.

Selbst, A. D. & Barocas, S. (2018). The Intuitive Appeal of Explainable Machines. *Fordham Law Review*, 87(3), 1085–1140.

Shindell, D. (2020). *Health and Economic Benefits of a 2°C Climate Policy, Testimony to the House Committee on Oversight and Reform Hearing on "The Devastating Impacts of Climate Change on Health,"* https://nicholas.duke.edu/sites/default/files/documents/Shindell_Testimony_July2020_final.pdf.

Shyy, S. (2021). The GDPR's Lose-Lose Dilemma: Minimal Benefits to Data Privacy & Significant Burdens on Business. *UC Davis Business Law Journal*, 20(2), 137–188.

Siddiqi, N. (2006). *Credit Risk Scorecards: Developing and Implementing Intelligent Credit Scoring*. Hoboken, NJ: John Wiley & Sons.

Siddiqi, N. (2016). *Intelligent Credit Scoring: Building and Implementing Better Credit Risk Scorecards*. 2nd ed., Somerset, KY: John Wiley & Sons, Incorporated.

Simkovic, M. & Furth-Matzkin, M. (2022). Pigouvian Contracts. *USC CLASS Research Paper*.

Sinden, A. (2015). Formality and Informality in Cost-Benefit Analysis. *Utah Law Review*, 2015(1), 93–172.

Smith, A. (2020). *Using Artificial Intelligence and Algorithms*, www.ftc.gov/business-guidance/blog/2020/04/using-artificial-intelligence-and-algorithms.

Solove, D. J. (2001). Privacy and Power: Computer Databases and Metaphors for Information Privacy. *Stanford Law Review*, 53(6), 1393–1462.

Solove, D. J. & Citron, D. K. (2018). Risk and Anxiety: A Theory of Data-Breach Harms. *Texas Law Review*, 96(4), 737–786.

Spinney, L. (2022). *Are We Witnessing the Dawn of Post-Theory Science?* www.theguardian.com/technology/2022/jan/09/are-we-witnessing-the-dawn-of-post-theory-science.

Stanford University Human-Centered Artificial Intelligence (2021). *Preliminary Comments on Proposed Rulemaking Under the California Privacy Rights Act Of 2020*, https://cppa.ca.gov/regulations/pdf/preliminary_rulemaking_comments_3.

Stone, D. (2011). *Policy Paradox: The Art of Political Decision Making*, 3rd ed., New York, London: W.W. Norton.

Sunstein, C. R. (2022). Governing by Algorithm? No Noise and (Potentially) Less Bias. *Duke Law Journal*, 71(6), 1175–1206.

Sutton, R. S. & Barto, A. G. (2019). *Reinforcement Learning: An Introduction*, 2nd ed., Cambridge, MA: MIT Press.

Technet (2023). *TechNet Highlights the Costs of a Patchwork of Privacy Laws on Consumers During National Data Privacy Week*, www.technet.org/media/technet-highlights-the-costs-of-a-patchwork-of-privacy-laws-on-consumers-during-national-data-privacy-week/#:~:text=A%202022%20study%20conducted%20by,billion%20footed%20by%20small%20businesses.

Terry, N. P. (2014). Big Data Proxies and Health Privacy Exceptionalism. *Health Matrix: Journal of Law-Medicine*, 24(6), 65–108.

The Treasury Department, The Comptroller of the Currency, The Federal Reserve System, The Federal Deposit Insurance Corporation, The Consumer Financial Protection Bureau, and The National Credit Union Administration (2021). *Request for Information and Comment on Financial Institutions' Use of Artificial Intelligence, Including Machine Learning*, Federal Register.

Thierer, A. (2013). A Framework for Benefit-Cost Analysis in Digital Privacy Debates. *George Mason Law Review*, 20(4), 1055–1106.

Tilly, C. (2006). *Why? What Happens When People Give Reasons ... And Why*, Princeton, NJ: Princeton University Press.

Topol, E. (2019). *Deep Medicine: How Artificial Intelligence Can Make Healthcare Human Again*, New York: Basic Books.

Tufekci, Z. (2019). *Think You're Discreet Online? Think Again*, www.nytimes.com/2019/04/21/opinion/computational-inference.html

U.S. Department of Health, Education & Welfare (1973). *Records Computers and the Rights of Citizens*, Cambridge, MA: The Massachusetts Institute of Technology.

Uršič, H. (2021). *Data Subject Rights under the GDPR*, Oxford: Oxford University Press.

Valentino-Devries, J., Singer-Vine, J., & Soltani, A. (2012). *Websites Vary Prices, Deals Based on Users' Information*, www.wsj.com/articles/SB10001424127887323777204578189391813881534.

Vanderstichele, G. (2019). *The Normative Value of Legal Analytics. Is There a Case for Statistical Precedent?* https://papers.ssrn.com/sol3/papers.cfm?abstract_id=3474878.

Wachter, S. (2022). The Theory of Artificial Immutability: Protecting Algorithmic Groups under Anti-Discrimination Law. *Tulane Law Review*, 97(2), 149–204.

Wachter, S., Floridi, L., & Mittelstadt, B. (2017). Why a Right to Explanation of Automated Decision-Making Does not Exist in the General Data Protection Regulation. *International Data Privacy Law*, 7(2), 76–99.

Walker, B. (2015). *Benjamen Walker's Theory of Everything*, https://theoryofeverythingpodcast.com/series/instaserfs/.

Walzer, M. (1983). *Spheres of Justice: A Defense of Pluralism and Equality*, New York: Basic Books.

Warner, M. R. (2019). *Senators Introduce Bipartisan Legislation to Ban Manipulative "Dark Patterns,"* www.warner.senate.gov/public/index.cfm/2019/4/senators-introduce-bipartisan-legislation-to-ban-manipulative-dark-patterns.

Williams, D. (2021). Problem Solved? Is the Fintech Era Uprooting Decades Long Discriminatory Lending Practices?. *Tulane Journal of Technology and Intellectual Property*, 23, 159–178.

Woods, A. K. (2022). Robophobia. *University of Colorado Law Review*, 93(1), 51–114.

Worker Info Exchange (2021). *Gig Workers Score Historic Digital Rights Victory against Uber & Ola*, www.workerinfoexchange.org/post/gig-workers-score-historic-digital-rights-victory-against-uber-ola-2.

Worker Info Exchange (2023). *Historic Digital Rights Win for WIE and the ADCU over Uber and Ola at Amsterdam Court of Appeal*, www.workerinfoexchange.org/post/historic-digital-rights-win-for-wie-and-the-adcu-over-uber-and-ola-at-amsterdam-court-of-appeal, April 4.

Wu, X. & Zhang, X. (2016). *Responses to Critiques of Machine Learning of Criminality Perceptions*, https://arxiv.org/abs/1611.04135.

Zax, D. (2012). *Fast Talk: How a Former Google Exec Plans to Transform Loans*, www.fastcompany.com/1813256/fast-talk-how-former-google-exec-plans-transform-loans.

Acknowledgments

I wish to thank Megan Richardson and Jeannie Paterson for their sterling guidance and advice as I wrote this Element. Their advice and support with respect to this project have been most valuable. Jing Qian has done an excellent job conforming the manuscript to Cambridge's exacting technical specifications, and I am grateful to her for this (and for a fascinating conversation on her important work illuminating the historical origins of contemporary privacy regulation).

Participants at the University of Utah's Faculty Workshop, the University of California at San Diego's Practical Ethics and Science Studies Workshop, Cornell Law School's Faculty Workshop, Cornell Tech's Digital Life Initiative, and two Automated Decisionmaking in Society Centre events in Melbourne offered informed and thoughtful feedback when I presented earlier versions of the argument to them. I also thank Ifeoma Ajunwa, Julie E. Cohen, Niklas Eder, Jake Goldenfein, Nikolas Guggenberger, Oreste Pollicino, Jeannie Paterson, Andrew Selbst, Michael Simkovic, Jay Varellas, and Ari Ezra Waldman for deeply insightful comments on drafts. I am grateful to Jeffrey Cheng, Melanie Condon, Daisy Fernandez, Max Goldstein, and Amina Rabi for their excellent research assistance.

Cambridge Elements

Data Rights and Wrongs

Megan Richardson
University of Melbourne

Megan Richardson is an Honorary Professor at the Melbourne Law School, the University of Melbourne. Her research covers privacy and data rights, law reform and legal theory. Her books include *The Right to Privacy: Origins and Influence of a Nineteenth-Century Idea* (2017); *Research Handbook on Intellectual Property in Media and Entertainment Law* (ed with Sam Ricketson, 2017); *Advanced Introduction to Privacy Law* (2020); and *The Right to Privacy 1914–1948: The Lost Years* (2023).

Rachelle Bosua
Deakin University

Rachelle Bosua is a Senior Lecturer at Deakin University and an Honorary Senior Fellow in the School of Computing and Information Systems at the University of Melbourne. She was previously an Assistant Professor at the Open University Netherlands. Her research considers the role and use of data in digital contexts, including data privacy and ethics, design and adoption of digital artefacts in remote and platform-based work, knowledge leakage and digital innovation. She is a co-author of *Knowledge Management in Organizations: A Critical Introduction* (with Donald Hislop and Remko Helms, 4th ed, 2018).

Damian Clifford
Australian National University

Damian Clifford is a Senior Lecturer in Law at the Australian National University and an associate researcher at the Information Law and Policy Centre at the Institute of Advanced Legal Studies (University of London). Previously a FWO Aspirant Fellow at KU Leuven's Centre for IT and IP Law (CiTiP), his research focuses on privacy, data protection and technology regulation, and he has published across these fields. His recent books are *Data Rights and Private Law* (ed with Jeannie Marie Paterson and Kwan Ho Lau, 2023) and *Data Protection Law and Emotions* (2024).

Jake Goldenfein
University of Melbourne

Jake Goldenfein is a Senior Lecturer at the Melbourne Law School, the University of Melbourne. Previously a researcher at Cornell Tech, Cornell University and New York Law School, his work spans media and communications history and theory, communications policy, privacy and media law. Current areas of focus are mechanism design, algorithmic transparency, and decision-making accountability. His book *Monitoring Laws: Profiling and Identity in the World State* was published in 2020.

Jeannie Marie Paterson
University of Melbourne

Jeannie Marie Paterson is Director of the Centre for AI and Digital Ethics at the University of Melbourne and a Professor of Law at the Melbourne Law School. Her research focuses on themes of support for vulnerable consumers; the regulation of new technologies in consumer and financial markets; and regulatory design for protecting consumer rights and promoting safe, fair and accountable technologies. Her recent books include *Misleading Silence* (ed with Elise Bant, 2020); and *Data Rights and Private Law* (ed with Damian Cliffordand Kwan Ho Lau, 2023)..

Julian Thomas
RMIT University

Julian Thomas is Director of the ARC Centre of Excellence for Automated Decision-Making and Society, and a Distinguished Professor in the School of Media and Communication at RMIT University in Melbourne. He has written widely about digital inclusion, automation and other topics relating to the pasts and futures of new communications and computing technologies. His books include *The Informal Media Economy* (2015); *Internet on the Outstation: The Digital Divide and Remote Aboriginal Communities* (2016); and *Wi-Fi* (with Ellie Rennie and Rowan Wilken, 2021).

Editorial Board

Mark Andrejevic, *Professor, Communications & Media Studies, Monash Data Futures Institute*
Sara Bannerman, *Professor, McMaster University, and Canada Research Chair in Communication Policy & Governance*
Claes Granmar, *Associate Professor, Faculty of Law, Stockholm University*
Sonia Katyal, *Associate Dean of Faculty Development & Research, Co-Director Berkeley Center for Law & Technology, Roger J Traynor Diistinguished Professor of Law, UC Berkeley*
Andrew Kenyon, *Professor of Law, Melbourne Law School, the University of Melbourne*
Orla Lynskey, *Professor of Law and Technology, University College London*
Frank Pasquale, *Professor of Law, Cornell Tech and Cornell Law School, New York*
Trisha Ray, *Associate Director and Resident Fellow, GeoTech Center, Atlantic Council*
Peggy Valcke, *Professor of Law & Technology and Vice-Dean of Research, Faculty of Law & Criminology, KU Leuven*
Normann Witzleb, *Associate Professor of Law, Chinese University of Hong Kong*

About the Series

This Cambridge Elements series provides a home for fresh arguments about data rights and wrongs along with legal, ethical and other responses. We encourage new ways of thinking about data as enmeshed within social, institutional and technical relations.

Cambridge Elements ≡

Data Rights and Wrongs

Elements in the Series

Data Rights in Transition
Rachelle Bosua, Damian Clifford, Jing Qian and Megan Richardson

Data Access and AI Explainability
Frank Pasquale

A full series listing is available at: www.cambridge.org/EDRW

For EU product safety concerns, contact us at Calle de José Abascal, 56–1°,
28003 Madrid, Spain or eugpsr@cambridge.org.

www.ingramcontent.com/pod-product-compliance
Lightning Source LLC
LaVergne TN
LVHW011854060526
838200LV00054B/4326

Forensic Linguistics in Southern Africa

Origins, Progress, and Prospects

Elements in Forensic Linguistics

DOI: 10.1017/9781009705172
First published online: November 2025

Russell H. Kaschula
University of the Western Cape

Monwabisi K. Ralarala
University of the Western Cape

Eliseu Mabasso
Eduardo Mondlane University

Zakeera Docrat
University of the Western Cape

Wellman Kondowe
Mzuzu University

Paul Svongoro
University of South Africa

Author for correspondence: Russell H. Kaschula, rrkaschula@uwc.ac.za

Abstract: This Element introduces the study of forensic linguistics, particularly in southern Africa, but also in Africa more generally. In the past six decades, there has been clear evidence that the discipline of forensic linguistics is, or was, unknown to general linguists, legal linguists, and applied linguists on the African continent. Now, however, the situation is rapidly changing, with forensic linguistics studies gaining momentum in various parts of Africa. In this Element, the authors introduce the topic, define the discipline, address the language of record issue in southern Africa, as well as critically debate the state of court interpreting and translation of documentation into African languages, address police interviewing techniques, while also looking at possible future developments in the discipline of forensic linguistics. This title is also available as Open Access on Cambridge Core.

Keywords: Southern Africa, forensic linguistics, origins, history, language of record

© Russell H. Kaschula, Monwabisi K. Ralarala, Eliseu Mabasso, Zakeera Docrat, Wellman Kondowe, and Paul Svongoro 2025

ISBNs: 9781009705202 (HB), 9781009705165 (PB), 9781009705172 (OC)
ISSNs: 2634-7334 (online), 2634-7326 (print)

Contents

	Series Preface	1
1	Introduction to African Forensic Linguistics	2
2	Language of Record and Proceedings in Southern Africa	9
3	Legal Interpreting in Southern Africa	19
4	An Overview of the Challenges in Police Investigative Interviewing in Multilingual Southern Africa	32
5	Forensic Linguistics in Southern Africa: Charting Future Directions	50
	References	61